FROM SEA ROUTES TO SILK ROADS

Fujian and the Ryukyu Kingdom

www.royalcollins.com

ILLUSTRATED FUJIAN AND THE MARITIME SILK ROAD

FROM SEA ROUTES TO SILK ROADS

Fujian and the Ryukyu Kingdom

Xie Chen & Lin Yanxi

Edited by Xie Bizhen

RC

Books Beyond Boundaries

ROYAL COLLINS

From Sea Routes to Silk Roads:
Fujian and the Ryukyu Kingdom

Xie Chen & Lin Yanxi
Edited by Xie Bizhen

Translated by Daniel McRyan

First published in 2023 by Royal Collins Publishing Group Inc.
Groupe Publication Royal Collins Inc.
BKM Royalcollins Publishers Private Limited

Headquarters: 550-555 boul. René-Lévesque O Montréal (Québec) H2Z1B1 Canada
India office: 805 Hemkunt House, 8th Floor, Rajendra Place, New Delhi 110 008

ISBN: 978-1-4878-1123-5

To find out more about our publications, please visit www.royalcollins.com.

Foreword

As early as the 1st century BC, China had established an entire sea route from Xuwen and Hepu of Guangdong Province in southeastern China to the east coast of India; however, the early Chinese navigation was rarely related to the country's economic development. Emperors launched navigations to seek either the elixir of immortality or overseas treasures to maintain the luxurious and decadent lifestyle in the palace. The real overseas trade of China commenced when the Bureau of Foreign Shipping was set up in the Tang Dynasty. It was not until then that overseas trade was included in the national fiscal revenue.

Thanks to its superior geographical condition, Fujian is destined to play a significant role in the history of the overseas transportation and trade of China.

When the Maritime Silk Road is mentioned today, the descriptions tend to paint an easy and poetic picture. However, the formation of the Maritime Silk Road in history has gone through years of thick and thin. The merciless sea had devoured countless lives before the winding Maritime Silk Road came into being. As we look back on its development, we must not forget those great pioneers, namely, the monks who crossed the sea, the common people who went to sea to scrape out a living, the soldiers who went to war abroad, the envoys who were sent overseas, the courtiers who took refuge in foreign countries, the survivors of the shipwrecks, and the crew of Zheng He, who led seven voyages to the West.

It was commonly believed that Fujian ships were the best of all in the Song Dynasty. It was because Fujian had the most advanced navigation and shipbuilding technology of the time that the Quanzhou port had tremendous prosperity. The compass was widely used in navigation and nautical astronomy was developed. The stars were the guide and the wind the fuel. Navigation guidebooks were written and maps were drawn and passed down for generations. The advanced Western technology was also widely adopted in the navigation of Fujian sailors, such as the hourglass and the telescope. Their concept of navigation was evolving rapidly. The saying that "the sea is where Fujian people farm" pinpoints that they sailed for economic benefits. And the leverage of the economy drove them to open the age of Chinese exploration, where voyages were made all over the world and goods shipped overseas.

As per the existing historical data, the footprints of Fujian maritime merchants have been found in Japan and the Korean Peninsula, Southeast Asia, South Asian countries and the African continent. Business people from foreign countries also took Fujian ports as their footholds of trade. Historical documents have recorded that foreign merchant vessels trading with Fujian came from Asia, Africa, Europe, and America. The ancient Maritime Silk Road of China was a joint construction by the people of all countries in the world.

We admire the perfection of the ancient Maritime Silk Road, scrutinize the history of the navigation of Fujian sailors, and respect the outstanding contribution of Fujian ancestors to China's navigation. Their extraordinary sailing activities have left us abundant treasure, such as the sunken ships in the deep ocean, the traded goods that were found everywhere, the harbors silent for many years, the vaguely recognizable buoys, the long navigation picture scrolls, the yellowing nautical guide manuals, and the Mazu temples. The compilation of the illustrated series *Fujian and the Maritime Silk Road* aims to gather these scattered historical fragments piece by piece, so that a full picture of the historical record of Fujian on the ancient Maritime Silk Road can be seen.

The history of the development of the ancient Maritime Silk Road has pinpointed that the Maritime Silk Road came into being thanks to both Chinese and the people of various countries and regions along the way. Now, China's proposal to jointly build the Maritime Silk Road of the 21st Century conforms to the trend of world multi-polarization, economic globalization, and social informatization. Conducive to promoting the orderly and free flow of economic elements, it conforms to the fundamental interests of both China and the international community, highlights the common ideal and pursuit of the human society, and will inject positive energy to the world development.

Reviewing the history of Fujian and the Maritime Silk Road enables us to understand that in the process of building the Maritime Silk Road of the 21st Century, China should make an effort to enhance its comprehensive national strength, develop a value system attractive to all countries, create real soft power, and build its international image and prestige, so as to gradually become a strong global influence.

We shall learn from the history of Fujian on the Maritime Silk Road, explore the secret of success, seize the opportunity, stride into a new era with confidence, and create a victorious future.

Xie Bizhen

Introduction

The Ryukyu Kingdom was an island kingdom located in the Pacific Ocean to the southeast of China (present-day Okinawa Prefecture of Japan), and its early history is little known. But what is certain is that the reign of King Satto began in 1350, and it was during this period that the Ming Dynasty government established formal diplomatic relations with the Ryukyu Kingdom.

It was stipulated in the early Ming Dynasty that there should be a bureau for foreign shipping to manage all foreign businessmen, and the Fujian bureau for foreign shipping was specially set up for the Ryukyu Kingdom. In the early Ming Dynasty, the Fujian bureau for foreign shipping was located in Quanzhou, and during the Chenghua period (1465–1487) of the Ming Dynasty, it was relocated to Fuzhou. The Ming Dynasty stipulated that Fujian be the only port connecting Ryukyu. From then on, the maritime communication between Fujian and the Ryukyu Kingdom has become an important part of the Fujian Maritime Silk Road.

Contents

CHAPTER 1

The Route from Fujian to the Ryukyu Kingdom

From the establishment of diplomatic relations between China and the Ryukyu Kingdom in 1372 to the annexation of the Ryukyu Kingdom by Japan in 1879, the relationship between China and the Ryukyu Kingdom lasted for over 500 years. During this period, Fujian was a critical stage. Historical data proves that as early as the late Southern Song Dynasty, the Fujianese had opened up a route to the Ryukyu Kingdom.

1 The Beginning and End of the Route

In the Song Dynasty, Fujian's shipbuilding industry was the most developed. Back then, there were ship factories in Zhangzhou, Quanzhou, Fuzhou, and Xinghua on the coast of Fujian, and it was famous for the locals who built ships and sailed abroad for business. During this period, as the compass was applied to navigation, and the mariner's compass appeared, which made navigation safer. The advancement of shipbuilding and navigation technology was an essential condition for the Fujian Maritime Silk Road to achieve unprecedented prosperity during the Song and Yuan Dynasties.

⦿ The Ancient City of Quanzhou

⊙ Ming Dynasty Laiyuanyi (department that used to manage foreigners) Site of Quanzhou

The contact between Fujian and the Ryukyu Kingdom started in Quanzhou. In the Ming Dynasty, Quanzhou was the largest port in the East. There was the Laiyuanyi, which managed foreign tourists from afar, the Bureau for Foreign Shipping, which managed overseas traffic and trade, and the Quanzhou Port, where merchant ships shuttled.

◉ Ancient Port of Quanzhou (present day)

In the reign of the Chenghua Emperor of the Ming Dynasty (1464–1487), Fuzhou became a vital port connecting the Ryukyu Kingdom. It was where the Chinese diplomatic corps departed China, and the Ryukyu diplomats entered China, which started the Sino-Ryukyu maritime trade history that lasted for centuries.

⊙ Panorama of the Ancient City of Fuzhou. It was drawn in 1684 by an anonymous painter, now collected in the Amsterdam Museum in the Netherlands.

◉ Fuzhou Wanshou Bridge in the Republic of China era (1911–1949)

⊙ Fuzhou Nantai Port in the Qing Dynasty (1636–1911)

◉ Ryukyu Naha Ancient Port in the Western works

In 1372, the Ryukyu Kingdom established formal diplomatic relations with Ming China as a tributary state of Imperial China and paid tribute to it annually.

◉ Map of the Ryukyu Kingdom

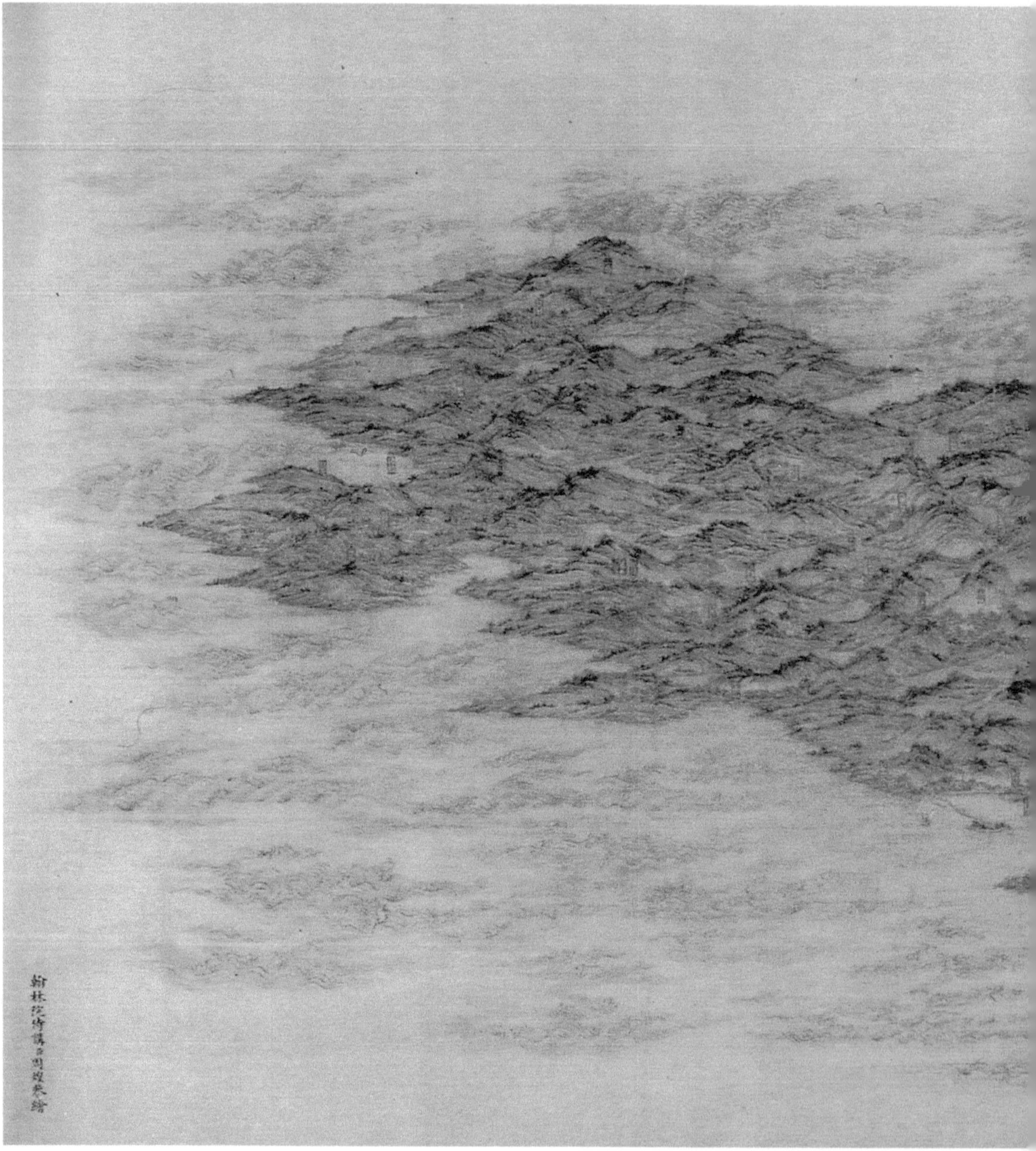

⊙ Map of the capital of the Ryukyu Kingdom

◉ Royal Palace Shuri of the Ryukyu Kingdom

From the Ryukyu Kingdom's establishment of tributary relations with Ming Dynasty, Fujian became a shipbuilding base. With the support of Fujian's shipbuilding industry, the maritime power of the Ryukyu Kingdom developed rapidly, making it a state with thriving maritime trade known as Wan Guo Jin Liang (a bridge to all countries).

The Wan Guo Jin Liang Bell was cast in 1458 and designated as a national cultural relic by the Japanese government in 1978. It now resides in the Okinawa Prefectural Museum.

◉ Wan Guo Jin Liang Bell

2 Sea Route Map between China and the Ryukyu Kingdom

The Fujianese opened up the China-Ryukyu route very early, and the sea route map between China and the Ryukyu Kingdom that has survived to this day is an accurate portrayal of the Fujianese sailing to the Ryukyu Kingdom.

Shun Feng Xiang Song is a sea route map composed by Fujian sailors in the Song and Yuan Dynasties based on long-term sailing experience. It describes the sea route from Fujian to the Ryukyu Kingdom. During the Yongle period (1403–1424) of the Ming Dynasty, Chinese officials repeatedly revised it according to their voyages to the West.

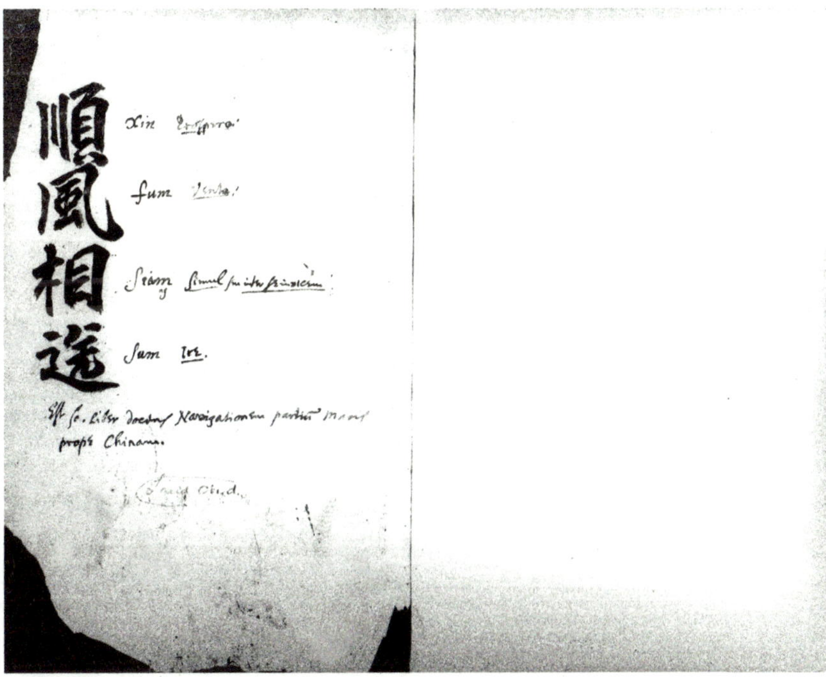

◉ *Shun Feng Xiang Song*, cover, sample page

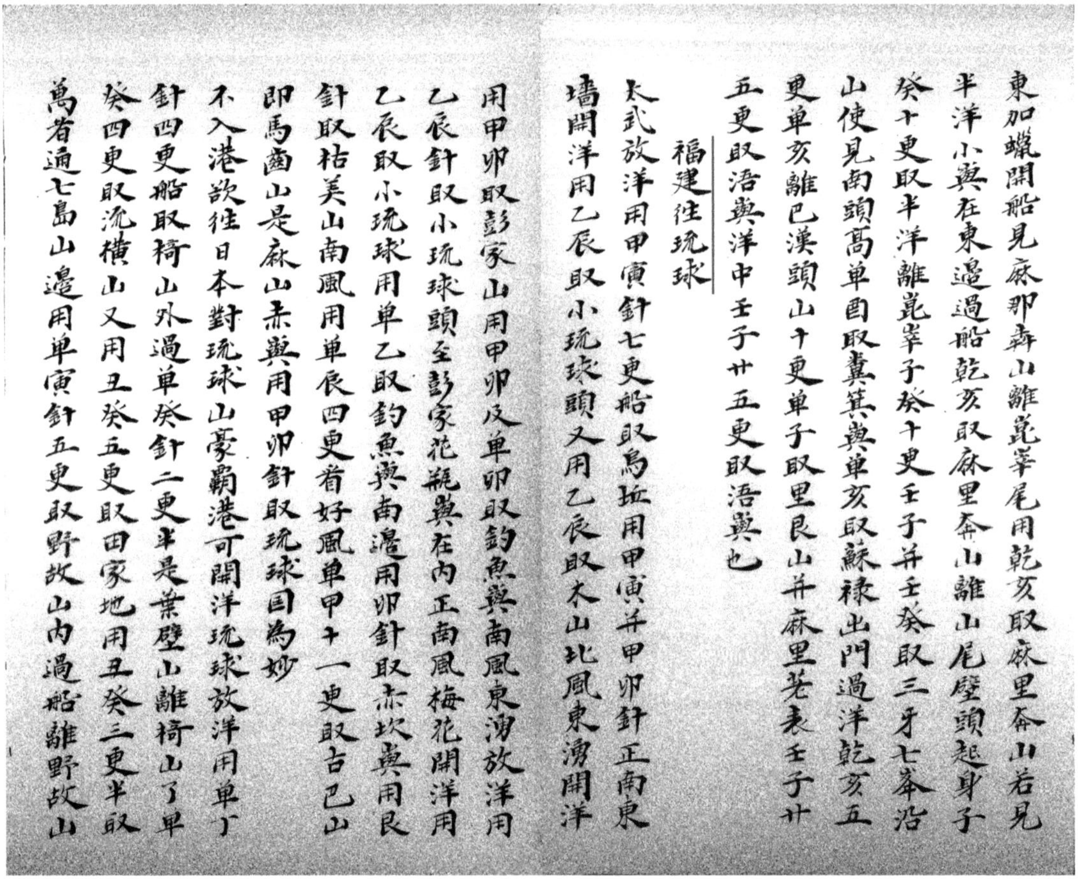

東加蠟開船見麻那番山離崑峯尾用乾亥取麻里奔山若見
半洋小嶼在東邊過船乾亥取麻里奔山離山尾壁頭起身子
癸十更取半洋離崑崙子癸十更壬子并壬癸取三牙七峯沿
山使見南頭高单酉取囊箕嶼单亥取蘇祿出門過洋乾亥五
更单亥離巴漢頭山十更单子取里艮山并麻里荖表壬子廿
五更取浯嶼洋中壬子廿五更取浯嶼也

福建往琉球

太武放洋用甲寅針七更船取烏坵用甲寅并甲卯針正南東
墻開洋用乙辰取小琉球頭又用乙辰取木山北風東湧開洋
用甲卯取彭家山用甲卯及单卯取釣魚嶼南風東湧放洋用
乙辰針取小琉球頭至彭家花瓶嶼在内正南風梅花開洋用
乙辰取小琉球用单乙取釣魚嶼南邊用卯針取赤坎嶼用艮
針取枯美山南風用单辰四更看好風单甲十一更取古巴山
即馬齒山是麻山赤嶼用甲卯針取琉球国為妙
不入港欲往日本對琉球山豪霸港可開洋琉球放洋用单丁
針四更船取椅山外過单癸針二更半是葉壁山離椅山了单
癸四更取流横山又用丑癸五更取田家地用丑癸三更半取
萬者通七島山邊用单寅針五更取野故山内過船離野故山

⦿ Records of the sea route from Fujian to the Ryukyu Kingdom in *Shun Feng Xiang Song*

Zhi Nan Guang Yi was written by Tei Junsoku of the Ryukyu Kingdom during the reign of the Qing Emperor Kangxi (1662–1722), according to Chinese nautical charts. Published in Fuzhou in 1708, it records the round-trip route from Fuzhou to the Ryukyu Kingdom.

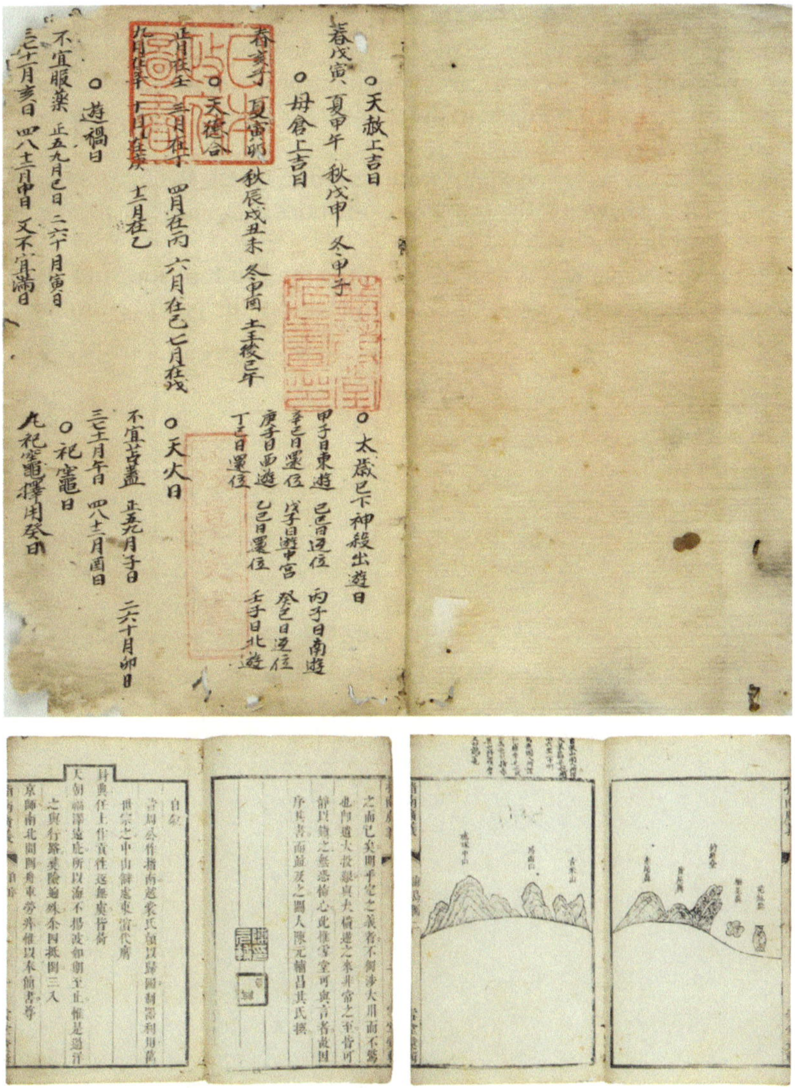

◉ *Zhi Nan Guang Yi*, sample page

3 Crossing the Sea to the Ryukyu Kingdom

During the Ming and Qing Dynasties, China conferred titles to the Ryukyu Kingdom 23 times, and every voyage for that purpose was recorded in detail. The nautical charts from Fujian to the Ryukyu Kingdom were also included in such records.

In 1579, Xiao Chongye and Xie Jie were accredited to the Ryukyu Kingdom. *The Ryukyu Records*, which they co-wrote, includes the painting *Crossing the Sea to the Ryukyu Kingdom.*

In 1719, Xu Baoguang was accredited to the Ryukyu Kingdom and wrote the book *Zhong Shan Chuan Xin Lu*, which includes the painting *Sea Route to the Ryukyu Kingdom.*

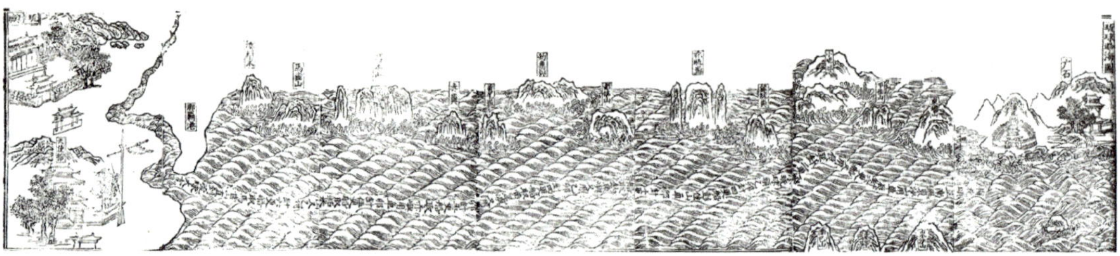

⦿ Xiao Chongye and Xie Jie, *Crossing the Sea to the Ryukyu Kingdom*

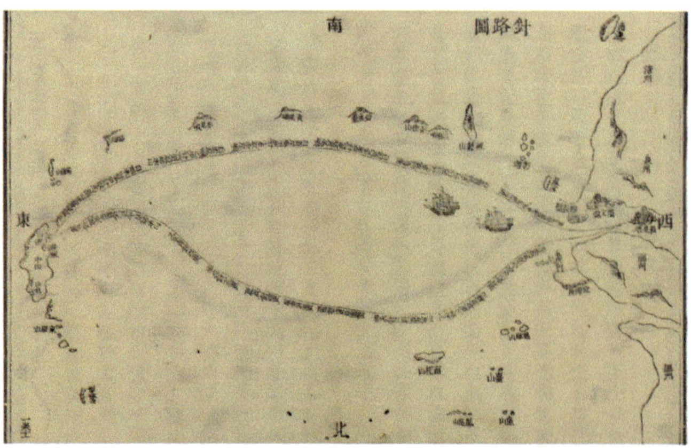

⦿ Xu Baoguang, *Sea Route to the Ryukyu Kingdom*

CHAPTER 2

Nautical Activities of Conferring Titles to the Ryukyu Kingdom

Conferring titles to the Ryukyu Kingdom was an important activity in the development of Sino-Ryukyu relations. And China's nautical activities of conferring titles to the Ryukyu Kingdom can be regarded as the most representative case of ancient Chinese voyages.

1 Conferring Titles to Ryukyu Envoys

The selection of Chinese envoys accredited to the Ryukyu Kingdom changed significantly from the Ming Dynasty to the Qing Dynasty. During the Yongle period (1403–1425) of the Ming Dynasty, the envoys were officials who had committed crimes and were punished to guard the borders. Next, as Sino-Ryukyu relations improved, the Ming court gradually paid more attention to the title bestowal, and most envoys were selected by the emperor himself.

During the Ming and Qing Dynasties, the Chinese envoys accredited to the Ryukyu Kingdom had to risk their lives to cross the sea. Some of them came from Fujian, and their historical traces can still be found today.

Guo Rulin (1510–1580) was a native of Yongfeng in Jiangxi Province. In April 1558, he was accredited to the Ryukyu Kingdom and handed Shō Gen his official investiture as king of the Ryukyu Kingdom. Guo Rulin, together with Li Jichun, authored *Recompiled Records of Being Sent to the Ryukyu Kingdom on Diplomatic Missions*.

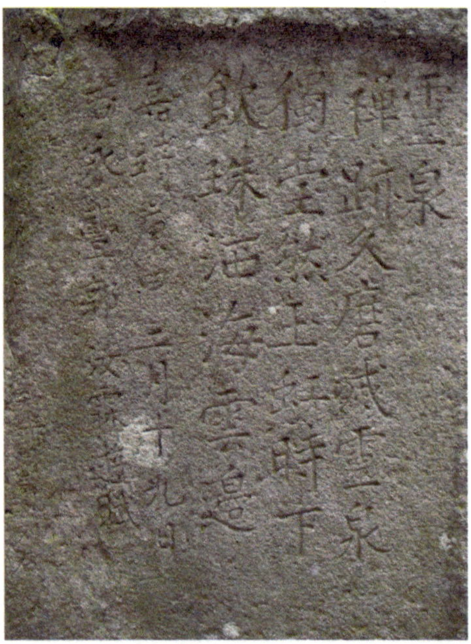

◉ Stone inscription about Guo Rulin in Gushan

Xie Jie (1535–1604) was a native of Fuzhou, Fujian Province. In 1579, he was accredited to the Ryukyu Kingdom. In addition to editing *Records of Being Sent to the Ryukyu Kingdom on Diplomatic Missions* with Xiao Chong, he also wrote *Summary Supplements to Records of the Ryukyu Kingdom (Trivial Notes)*, which was included in the appendix of *Records of Being Sent to the Ryukyu Kingdom on Diplomatic Missions* by Xia Ziyang.

Qi Kun (?–1814) was a native of Fuzhou, Fujian Province. In 1808, he was accredited to the Ryukyu Kingdom. He authored *Continuing the History of the Ryukyu Kingdom* and *Hundred Odes of Japan*. In particular, the eight odes of navigation during his diplomatic mission in the Ryukyu Kingdom vividly depict the voyages between China and the Ryukyu Kingdom.

Zhao Xin (1809–1876) was a native of Fuzhou, Fujian Province. In 1866, he was accredited to the Ryukyu Kingdom, which was the last time the Chinese government sent envoys to confer titles to the Ryukyu Kingdom. And he wrote the *Sequel to the History of the Ryukyu Kingdom*.

◉ Xie Jie's tomb site

◉ Qi Kun's epitaph

◉ Zhao Xin's Tombstone

2 Documents of the Voyages to Confer Titles to the Ryukyu Kingdom

When conferring titles to the Ryukyu Kingdom, China kept over 20 kinds of diplomatic records, which describe the shipbuilding and navigation activities for such title bestowal.

According to historical records, the Ryukyu Kingdom started to receive official investiture from China starting in the Ming Dynasty. In 1372, Satto, King of Chūzan in the Ryukyu Kingdom, accepted the amnesty and enlistment of the Ming Dynasty and formally established diplomatic relations with China.

In 1404, the Ming Dynasty sent envoys to the Ryukyu Kingdom to pay tribute to Satto, the last King of Chūzan, and crowned Bunei as the new king. This was the beginning of the title bestowal to Ryukyu. After that, the Ryukyu Kingdom received grand official investitures by the Ming and Qing Dynasties until it was annexed by Japan in 1879.

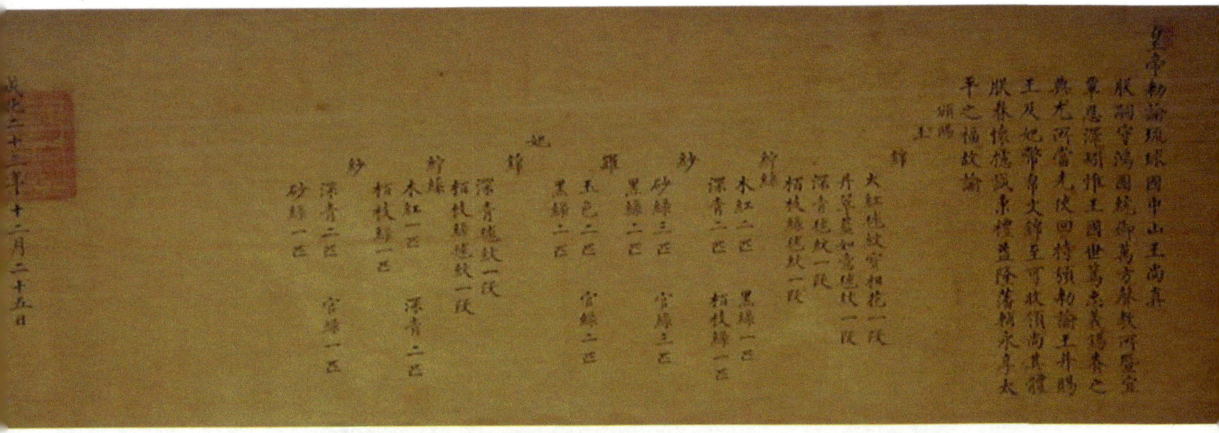

⊙ The imperial edict of Dong Min and Zhang Xiang being accredited to the Ryukyu Kingdom during the Chenghua period (1464–1487) of the Ming Dynasty, now collected in the Okinawa Prefectural Museum, Japan

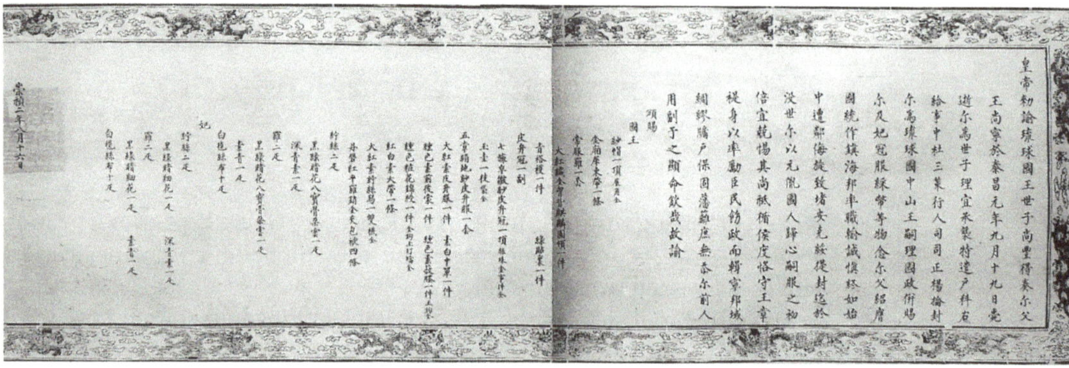

The imperial edict of Du Sance being accredited to the Ryukyu Kingdom during the Chongzhen Period (1627–1644) of the Ming Dynasty

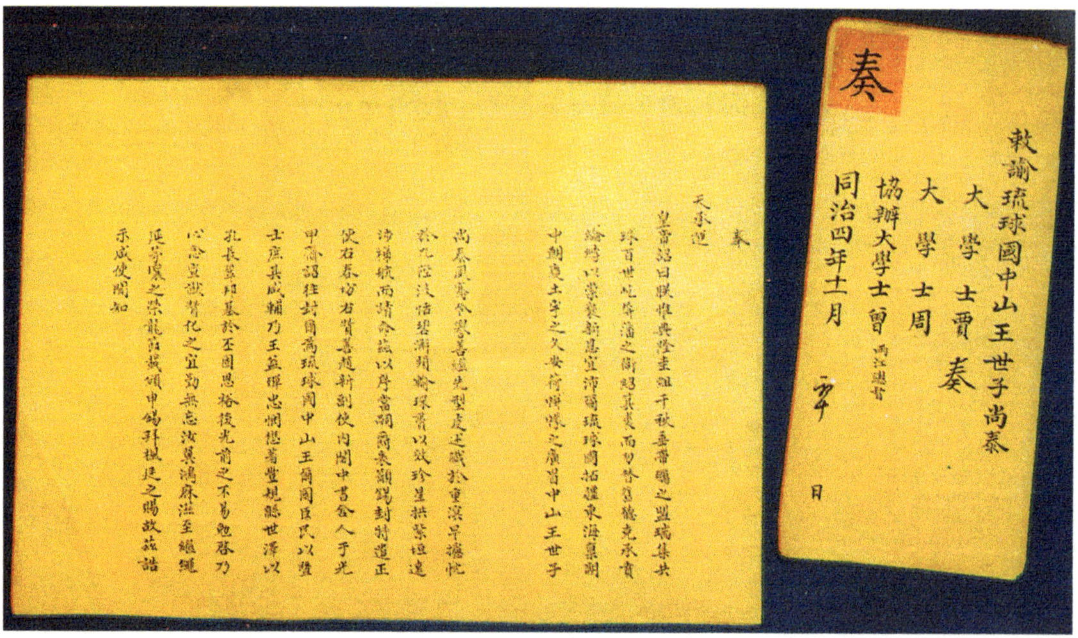

The imperial edict of Zhao Xin being accredited to the Ryukyu Kingdom during the Tongzhi Period (1861–1875) of the Qing Dynasty

a. A description of the Imperial Chinese envoys in the Ming and Qing Dynasties

In the Ming and Qing dynasties, after returning home from the Imperial Chinese missions to the Ryukyu kingdom were complete, the envoys had to write down their experience in the Ryukyu kingdom and report it to the emperor. Later, their mission records were published. Among them was the earliest publication, *Records of Imperial Missions to the Ryukyu Kingdom,* by Chen Kan in 1534.

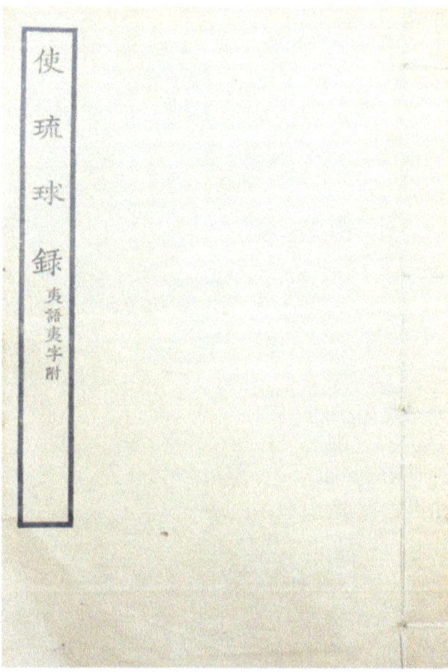

◉ Chen Kan's *Records of Imperial Missions to the Ryukyu kingdom*, cover, sample page

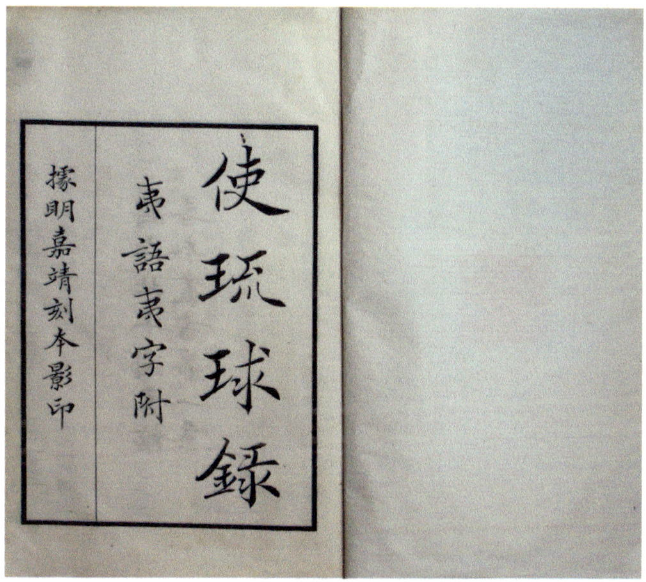

◉ Chen Kan's *Records of Imperial Missions to the Ryukyu kingdom*, first page, sample page

Wang Ji (1626–1689) was a native of Xiuning, Anhui Province. In 1683, he was accredited to the Ryukyu Kingdom. After returning to China, he wrote *Evolution of Chūzan, The Sequence Diagram of the First Kings and Gods of the Ryukyu Kingdom*, and *Miscellaneous Records of Imperial Missions to the Ryukyu Kingdom*. And *Evolution of Chūzan*, as the first Ryukyu history book by a Chinese, recorded important information about the voyages from Fujian to Ryukyu and the Diaoyu Islands.

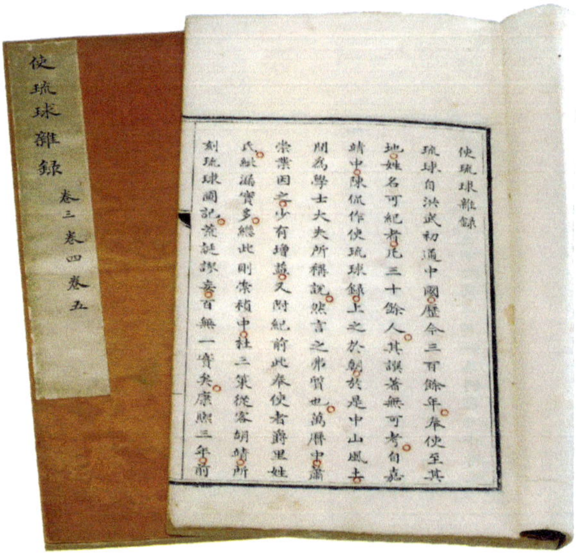

⦿ *Miscellaneous Records of Imperial Missions to the Ryukyu Kingdom* by Wang Ji

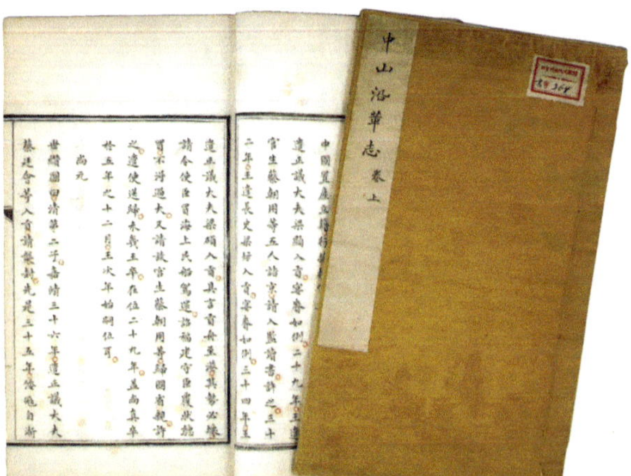

⦿ *Evolution of Chūzan* by Wang Ji

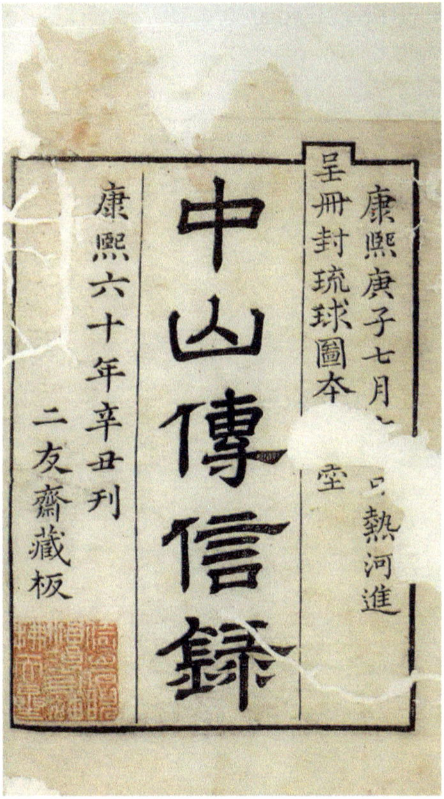

Xu Baoguang (1671–1740) was a native of Wu County, Jiangsu Province. In 1719, he and Wang Shangjing were accredited to the Ryukyu Kingdom and stayed there for eight months, which was the longest stay for Chinese in the Ryukyu Kingdom. Xu Baoguang wrote the book *Zhong Shan Chuan Xin Lu* after returning to Imperial China, which is the most detailed record of Imperial Chinese missions among all documents by Chinese envoys to the Ryukyu Kingdom.

⦿ *Zhong Shan Chuan Xin Lu* by Xu Baoguang, sample page

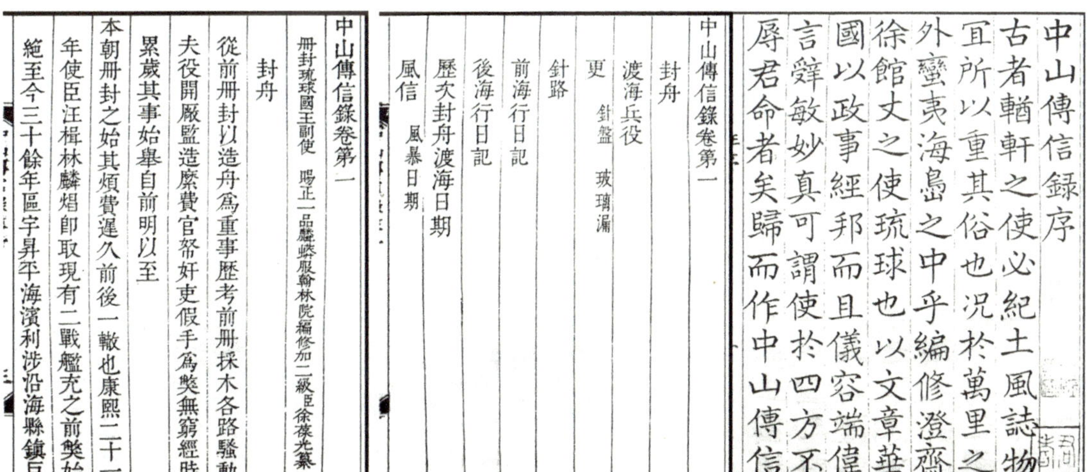

中山傳信錄序
古者輶軒之使必紀土風誌物
宜所以重其俗也況於萬里之
外蠻夷海島之中乎編修澄齋
徐館丈之使琉球也以文章華
國以政事經邦而且儀容端偉
言辭敏妙真可謂使於四方不
辱君命者矣歸而作中山傳信

中山傳信錄卷第一
封舟
渡海兵役
更　針盤　玻璃漏
針路
前海行日記
後海行日記
歷次封舟渡海日期
風信　風暴日期

中山傳信錄卷第一
冊封琉球國王副使　賜正一品麟蟒服翰林院編修加二級臣徐葆光纂
封舟
從前冊封以造舟為重事歷考前冊採木各路騷動
夫役開廠監造縻費官帑奸吏假手為奬無窮經時
累歲其事始舉自前明以至
本朝冊封之始其煩費遲久前後一轍也康熙二十一
年使臣汪楫林麟焻卽取現有二戰艦充之前奬始
絕至今三十餘年區宇昇平海濱利涉沿海縣鎮巨

Zhou Huang (1714–1785) was a native of Fuling, Chongqing (then-Sichuan Province). In 1756, he was sent to the Ryukyu Kingdom as an envoy. After the mission ended, he wrote *History of the Ryukyu Kingdom*.

In addition, Qi Kun, sent to the Ryukyu Kingdom as an envoy in 1808, wrote *Sequel to the History of the Ryukyu Kingdom* after his trip.

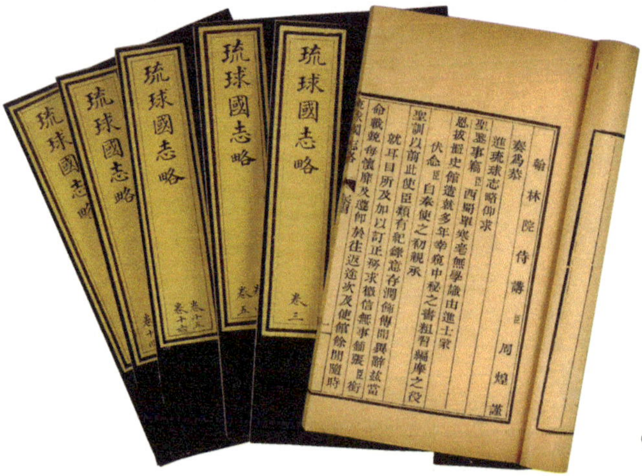

◉ *History of the Ryukyu Kingdom* by Zhou Huang, sample page

◉ *Sequel to the History of the Ryukyu Kingdom* by Qi Kun, sample page

b. Local Fujianese literature related to the Ryukyu Kingdom

The History of the Fujian Bureau for Foreign Shipping is a chronicle about the Fujian Bureau for Foreign Shipping in the Ming Dynasty. It records the evolution of Fujian Bureau for Foreign Shipping. It is an important document for the study of the Fujian foreign shipping system and the trade between Fujian and the Ryukyu Kingdom in the Ming Dynasty.

The Fujian Coastal Navigation Matters Archives (transcript) contains the archives of the Fujian local government in the Qing Dynasty that are mainly related to the regulations on shipbuilding and ship operations along the coast of Fujian, the travel of the imperial mission ships to the Ryukyu Kingdom in 1800 and matters of trade.

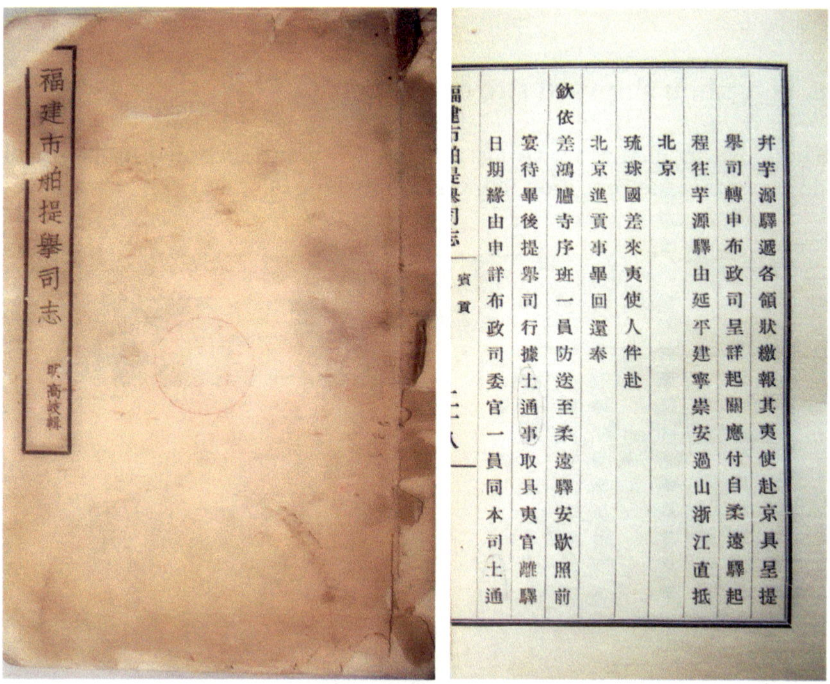

福建市舶提舉司志

明 高岐 輯

并芋源驛遞各領狀繳報其夷使赴京具呈提
舉司轉申布政司呈詳起關應付自柔遠驛起
程往芋源驛由延平建寧崇安過山浙江直抵
北京
琉球國差來夷使人件赴
北京進貢事畢回還奉
欽依差鴻臚寺序班一員防送至柔遠驛安歇照前
宴待畢後提舉司行據土通事取具夷官離驛
日期緣由申詳布政司委官一員同本司土通

福建市舶提舉司志 賓貢

⊙ *History of Fujian Bureau for Foreign Shipping*, sample page

3 Shipbuilding and Navigation for the Imperial Missions to the Ryukyu Kingdom

Regarding the imperial missions to the Ryukyu Kingdom, shipbuilding was paramount. The imperial envoys put great effort into the selection of shipbuilding materials and shipbuilders.

The imperial mission ships to the Ryukyu Kingdom were usually built in Fujian. Shipbuilders came from all over the province, among which those from Quanzhou and Zhangzhou were the first to be recruited. Shipbuilding materials were collected throughout Fujian Province and transported to Fuzhou.

a. Fengzhou shipyard site of Fuzhou

The most detailed Ming Dynasty shipbuilding site recorded in historical documents is the Fengzhou Shipyard of Fuzhou.

⊙ Nantai Sheren Temple shipbuilding site of Fuzhou

b. Imperial mission ships

During the Ming and Qing dynasties, every new king of the Ryukyu Kingdom had to request the Imperial Chinese government to send envoys to bestow the title. The ship that carried the envoys across the sea was called a *fengzhou* (imperial mission ships), and its construction was exquisite, as recorded in *Zhong Shan Chuan Xin Lu* by Xu Baoguang.

◉ *Fengzhou* ship

◉ *Fengzhou* ships arriving

c. The imperial mission voyages to the Ryukyu Kingdom

The Imperial Chinese envoys sent to the Ryukyu Kingdom used to set off from Nantai in Fuzhou, and local officials in Fujian had to see them off at the port. The seeing-off ceremony was solemn, including burning incense to offer a sacrifice to Heaven, inviting the sea god for a feast, and reciting prayers for safe sailing. Next, the imperial mission ships sailed onto the vast sea with the blessings of coastal soldiers.

◉ Boarding the Imperial Mission Ship to the Ryukyu Kingdom during the Qianlong Period (1736–1795) of the Qing Dynasty

The voyages to confer titles to the Ryukyu Kingdom always set sail in summer, riding the southwest wind, and returned when winter arrived, riding the northeast wind. The imperial envoys checked the number of passengers at the post in Nantai, Fuzhou, and made sure all boarded the ships. Riding the tide, they sailed straight towards the estuary of the Min River.

◉ *Boarding the ship in Fuzhou* in *Envoys to the Ryukyu Kingdom Scroll*

The Luoxing Pagoda, located at the estuary of Fuzhou, has always been a navigation mark for passing ships. As the seawater is salty and inedible, a large amount of fresh water had to be prepared on the mission ships, which were specially equipped with water tanks. During every mission voyage to the Ryukyu Kingdom, a water collection ceremony was held when ships reached Luoxing Pagoda. After burning incense and worshipping, the water tanks on the ships were filled with fresh water.

⦿ *Water Collection at Luoxing Pagoda* in *Envoys to the Ryukyu Kingdom Scroll*

Before setting off for the imperial mission to the Ryukyu Kingdom, it was usually necessary to recite two verses to prayers to the sea gods for their blessings. The prayers to the sea gods used to be written by Hanlin Academy, as requested by the Ministry of Rites after the envoys for the imperial mission to the Ryukyu Kingdom were selected. In the Ming and Qing dynasties, the content of such prayers differed little.

◉ *Pray to the Sea Gods* in *Envoys to the Ryukyu Kingdom Scroll*

There was Min'an Town near the estuary of the Min River in Fuzhou. It was where the *yamen* (local government office) of the Inspection Department was located. It was set to escort the ships to the sea and manage the foreign ships entering the port—mainly those from the Ryukyu Kingdom. A *fengzhou* was usually anchored in the nearby Yishanyuan, and after the *yamen* of the Inspection Department sent officers to make sure the safety of the sea area, they would notify the mission envoys that it was safe to sail.

◉ *Min'an Inspection Officers* in *Envoys to the Ryukyu Kingdom Scroll*

At the estuary of the Min River in Fuzhou, there are five reefs that look like five tigers, squatting and watching the vast sea. They used to be the natural beacons for navigation at sea. After a long voyage, sailors would know they had arrived in Fuzhou as soon as they saw the Five Tiger Reef. Also, when the imperial ships sailed past the Five Tiger Reef and exited the estuary of the Min River, every passenger understood that a life-and-death voyage had begun.

◉ *Five Tiger Reef* in *Envoys to the Ryukyu Kingdom Scroll*

On the route between China and the Ryukyu Kingdom, there is a dark trough, which is the border between them. Every time the ships reached the dark trough, envoys would throw live pigs and live sheep and make libations as sacrifices.

◉ *Crossing the Dark Trough at Midnight* in *Envoys to the Ryukyu Kingdom Scroll*

Navigation in ancient times relied on the monsoons as a driving force. Also, the ocean currents were an important factor. Regarding the imperial mission in the Ryukyu Kingdom, after passing the dark trough, the ocean current flowed from the Taiwan Straits to the Sea of Japan, greatly accelerating the voyages. Usually, it took more than ten days to sail from

Fuzhou to Ryukyu, and when the weather worked against the voyage, it could take up to a month. But when the wind and the ocean helped, in 1683, it took only three days for the diplomatic corps led by Wang Ji to reach the Ryukyu Kingdom, which was incredible. And the ancients attributed this miracle to the divine power of Mazu.

⦿ *Thousands of Li Down the Wind* in *Envoys to the Ryukyu Kingdom Scroll*

Kume refers to the most southwestern island in the Ryukyu Kingdom, also known as Kume Mountain and now called Kume Island. In the history of Sino-Ryukyu voyages, many documents record that the Ryukyu locals cheered on the ship when they laid eyes on Kume Island, screaming, "We are home!" There are many reefs around the island, so if passing ships arrived at the island at night, they would not dare to approach it recklessly but would have to wait until dawn to move forward.

◉ *Arriving at Kume Island* in *Envoys to the Ryukyu Kingdom Scroll*

When *fengzhou* ships crossed the ocean, they often stopped to wait when the wind blew in the wrong direction, and sometimes they lost their direction and sailed towards Japan. When that happened, they had to wait for the wind to blow them back to the Ryukyu Kingdom.

Waiting for the Wind in *Envoys to the Ryukyu Kingdom Scroll*

The route between China and Ryukyu was challenging and perilous, and most of the Imperial Chinese envoys were ready to sacrifice their lives when they set off on the journey. Because all imperial mission ships to the Ryukyu Kingdom were built in Fuzhou and experienced sailors were recruited, despite the peril along the route between China and the Ryukyu Kingdom, *fengzhou* ships survived every crisis.

◉ *Surviving the Danger* in *Envoys to the Ryukyu Kingdom Scroll*

The diplomatic corps used to wait for the wind in Kume, and when the monsoon was favorable for the voyage, they would hoist their sails and continue to move forward.

⦿ *Hoist Sail from Kume* in *Envoys to the Ryukyu Kingdom Scroll*

When *fengzhou* ships anchored at Naha Port in the Ryukyu Kingdom, the king of the Ryukyu Kingdom led scores of officials to greet the envoys, and citizens gathered on the road. Ryukyu officials would greet the envoys one by one. After courtesies were exchanged, the envoys would move to the Hall of Imperial Envoys to rest.

⦿ *Entry and Landing* in *Envoys to the Ryukyu Kingdom Scroll*

The ancient Chinese rulers believed that the deceased should be commemorated before the title bestowal, which is about loyalty and filial piety, so the Chinese diplomatic corps in the Ryukyu Kingdom would first hold the sacrificial ceremony before conferring titles.

⊙ *Commemorate the Former King of Envoys to the Ryukyu Kingdom* Scroll

After the ritual, the bestowal ceremony was held on a selected day. When that was over, the envoys returned to the embassy, waiting for the wind to return to Imperial China.

◉ *The Proclamation of Imperial Edict in* the *Envoys to the Ryukyu Kingdom* Scroll

As customary, the envoys had to attend seven banquets of the king during their stay in the Ryukyu Kingdom. They were often invited by the king to visit famous temples and historic sites. People from all walks of life in the two states would also exchange views on various issues to enhance mutual understanding and further consolidate their friendship.

Before the Imperial Chinese envoys embarked on the return to their motherland, they had first to invite the statues of the Queen of Heaven and Shangshu to the ships. On the day of boarding the ships, the king of the Ryukyu Kingdom led scores of officials to send them off, reluctant to part.

◉ *Boarding of the Ship Home* in *Envoys to the Ryukyu Kingdom Scroll*

When the *fengzhou* ships departed Naha Port, usually following the ocean current, they would enter Zhejiang waters and then go south along the coast, enter the Dinghai Bay of Lianjiang, and sail into the Min River estuary under the escort of the Fujian Navy.

◉ *Return* in *Envoys to the Ryukyu Kingdom Scroll*

When the envoys were on their way home, the Fujian navy dispatched sailors to inquire at sea every day. Once they heard from the envoys, they would report the news to the government. After a short rest in Fuzhou, the envoys had to rush to the capital to report, which would take another two months.

⊙ *Ships Arrived in Fuzhou* in *Envoys to the Ryukyu Kingdom Scroll*

d. The marching diplomatic corps to the Ryukyu Kingdom

The etiquette bestowing titles was very particular. In the Qing Dynasty, for example, when the envoys took the order from the capital, they followed the custom of going to the relevant department to receive a set of instruments for the trip to the Ryukyu Kingdom. When preparing for the title bestowal after arrival, the Chinese envoys and the Ryukyu officials responsible for the title bestowal discussed the ceremony procedures in detail together. There are no more title bestowals from China to the Ryukyu Kingdom today. But fortunately, there are pictures of the ceremony that have been passed down, which allow us to catch a glimpse of the grand team that traveled to the Ryukyu Kingdom for the imperial mission at that time. This long scroll of marching vassals, which is now in the Okinawa Prefectural Museum in Japan, is a historical witness to the friendship between China and the Ryukyu Kingdom.

令
令

廻避
肅靜
廻避
肅靜

清道
清道

◉ Ryukyu Palace antique worship ceremony

◉ Antique worship ceremony: the law officer offers incense

◉ Antique worship ceremony: the king leaves the hall

◉ Antique worship ceremony: the king pays his respect

4 Belief in Sea Gods

During the imperial voyages to the Ryukyu Kingdom, the main sea god worshipped was Mazu, and at the same time, gods such as Lady Linshui, the Sea Dragon King, Na Tuk Kong, Chen Wenlong, and Su Chen were also enshrined. In the coastal areas of Fujian and Okinawa, Japan, there are rich historical relics of the religious beliefs of China and the Ryukyu Kingdom.

a. Shangshu Temple of Taijiang

Wanshou Shangshu Temple in Fuzhou used to be located beside the Wanshou Bridge in the Taijiang District (relocated to the Xiahang intersection due to urban construction). It was built during the Yongle Period (1402–1424) of the Ming Dynasty. And the lord god worshipped is Chen Wenlong.

Chen Wenlong was born in Putian, Fujian. In 1370, he was appointed the Minister of Waters, and the people in the Fuzhou area worshiped him as the god of water, and many temples were built to honor him. Both Fujianese and Ryukyu people believed in Chen Wenlong, as confirmed by the inscription in the Shangshu Temple of Fuzhou.

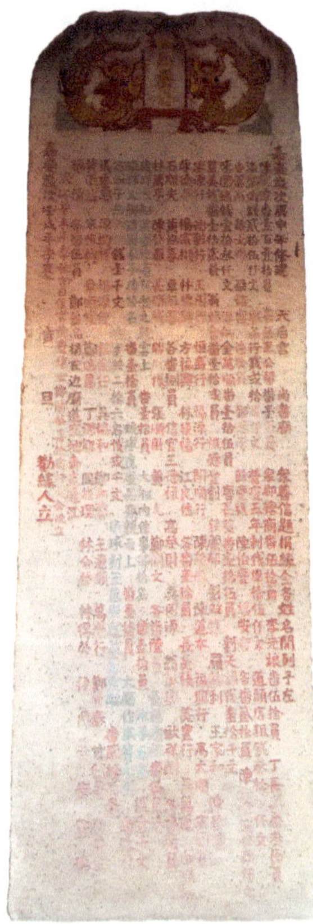

◉ Monument donated by the Ryukyu people in the Shangshu Temple of Fuzhou

◉ Part of the Shangshu Temple Monument of Fuzhou

b. Lady Linshui Temple

Lady Linshui Chen Jinggu is a goddess worshipped by Fujianese and Taiwanese. She died praying for rain to fight drought and to remove the evils of the people. Thus, people see her as the god of saving agriculture and safeguarding fertility and also the goddess of the sea, who, together with Mazu, blesses and protects the sailors.

◉ Lady Linshui Temple at Tating, Fuzhou

c. Yishanyuan Thean Hou Temple

Yishanyuan is located in the Tingjiang Middle School, Tingjiang Town, Mawei District, Fuzhou City. It was built in the early Qing Dynasty. From 1719 to 1866, the imperial mission envoys held ceremonies here to worship the Queen of Heaven before and after their voyage.

◉ Yishanyuan Temple of Tingjiang, Fuzhou

d. Tianfei Temple of Wenshi

Tianfei Temple of Wenshi is located in Wenshi Village, Tantou Town, Changle District, Fuzhou City. It was built in 1409. In the Ming Dynasty, before the Chinese envoys sent to the Ryukyu Kingdom set sail, they held rituals offering sacrifices to the sea god there, and it was also where the local officials of Fujian saw them off.

◉ Site of Tianfei Temple of Wenshi

e. Lady Cai Temple of Meihua, Changle

The deeds and legends about Lady Cai of Ryukyu are recorded in the *Cai Family Tree* and the *Chinese Changle County Chronicle*. During the long-term exchanges between China and the Ryukyu Kingdom, she became the protector of the voyages between China and the Ryukyu Kingdom. The Lady Cai Temple is located in Meixi Village, Meihua Town, Changle District, Fuzhou City.

◉ Lady Cai Temple of Meihua, Changle

◉ Statue of Lady Cai

f. Tianfei Palace and Guanyin Temple in the Ryukyu Kingdom

Due to the limitations of ancient seamanship, ships were often in peril. When people were rescued at sea, around them were always floating wooden statues that fell into the water with them, which convinced people that their survival from the disaster was purely the blessing of the gods. Therefore, people built temples where they were rescued to worship these gods. Since the transportation between Imperial China and the Ryukyu Kingdom was connected, survivors of sunken ships appeared from time to time. The survivors who drifted along the current from Fujian to Ryukyu have brought many religious beliefs to the Ryukyu locals, such as the belief in Tianfei and Guanyin.

◉ The Tianfei Temple on Kume Island before World War II

◉ Tianfei comes to the rescue

◉ Portrait of Ryukyu Guanyin painted by Westerners

◉ Guanyin Temple of Yaeyama, Ryukyu

5 Remains of Artifacts Related to the Voyages between Imperial China and the Ryukyu Kingdom

There are plenty of stories about the voyages between Imperial China and the Ryukyu Kingdom. The nautical compasses, the fortune-telling books, the mountains and rivers, the beacons, and the water villages are all branded with deep historical marks.

In the early Ming Dynasty, the Ryukyu Kingdom was an economically backward state. Although it was an island state, its seafaring power was rather weak. It was unable to engage in foreign traffic and trade activities. Since the establishment of diplomatic relations with the Ming court, the Fujian Bureau for Foreign Shipping took charge of the trade and foreign affairs of the Ryukyu Kingdom. After that, Fujian's navigation and shipbuilding technology deeply affected the history of its marine development.

The Chinesc invented the compass and used it in navigation. Its advent was a major breakthrough in ancient navigation history. Its use in navigation by both Imperial China and the Ryukyu Kingdom in the Ming and Qing Dynasties has been recorded in many documents.

An ancient nautical compass, now in the Taketomi Island Folk Custom Museum, Ishigaki Island, Okinawa, Japan

Yu Xia Ji Tong Shu Guang Ji is a book about fengshui customs. It is now in the Yaeyama Museum on Ishigaki Island, Okinawa, Japan. It was purchased by a Yaeyama local in Fuzhou during the Guangxu period (1871–1908) of the Qing Dynasty.

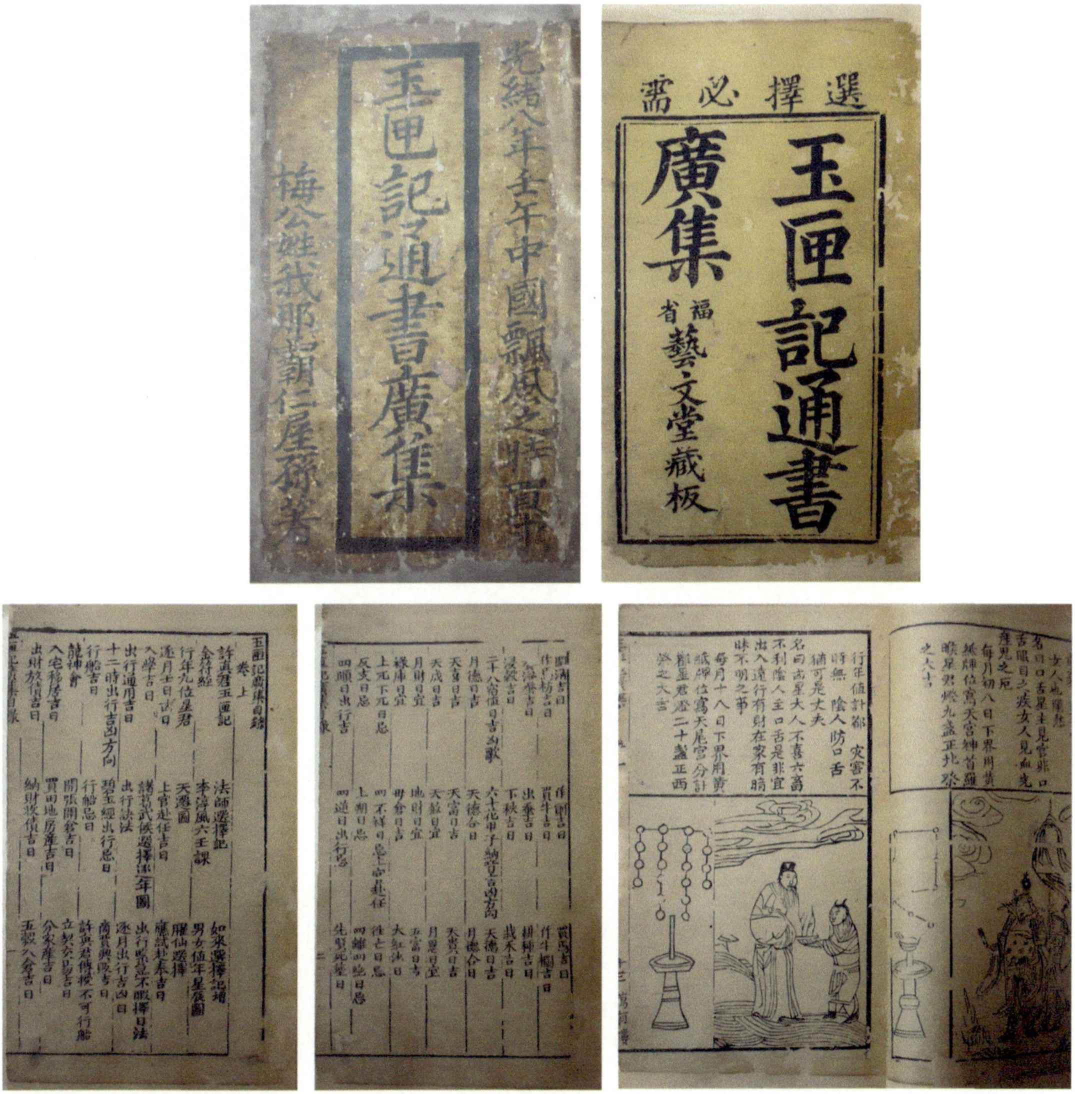

⊙ *Yu Xia Ji Tong Shu Guang Ji*, sample page

The Five Tiger Reefs, nautical markings of the Min River Estuary, are recorded in the *Diary of Sulphur Mining* by Yu Yonghe, a geographer in the Qing Dynasty. The name Five Tigers is often mentioned in Zheng He's nautical charts, the accounts of Chinese envoys sent to the Ryukyu Kingdom in successive dynasties, and the nautical documents of the Ryukyu Kingdom.

⦿ Five Tiger Reefs in Min River Estuary

Dinghai Bay of Lianjiang is actually the outer port of Fuzhou. All ships from the Ryukyu Kingdom to Fuzhou, including those imperial mission ships, sailed downwind to the sea from Wenzhou in Zhengjiang when returning to Fuzhou, and then south into Dinghai Bay of Lianjiang. And many Ryukyu shipwreck survivors were taken there by the raging winds.

⦿ Dinghai Bay of Lianjiang

In the Ming Dynasty, on the sea route of the Min River, the Meihua Institute of Changle District in Fuzhou City and the Wanan Institute in Fuqing City played a vital role. Soldiers from there were often selected to sail alongside the imperial mission envoys to the Ryukyu Kingdom because they were adept at sailing from an early age. They were necessary for escorting the envoys to the destination.

◉ (LEFT) Meihua Institute of Changle District

◉ (BELOW) Wanan Institute of Fuqing City

CHAPTER 3

Maritime Trade Between Fujian and the Ryukyu Kingdom

There are very few records of ancient China's overseas trade, and even in the works devoted to recording overseas trade, there are merely 200+ types of overseas trade commodities. But surprisingly, thousands of items in the nautical trade between Fujian and Ryukyu are well documented, which suggests the prosperity of overseas trade between Fujian and the Ryukyu Kingdom in ancient times.

1 The Fujian Bureau for Foreign Shipping and Ryukyu-Kan

In the early Ming Dynasty, the Fujian Bureau for Foreign Shipping was established to manage trade with the Ryukyu Kingdom. Following the Ming system, in the Qing Dynasty, Fujian remained the only port connecting Ryukyu, and there are still many historical sites about the Ryukyu tribute and trade.

Min'an Town stands about 35 kilometers away from Fuzhou. The rivers there are narrow and deep, making Min'an the thoroughfare of Fujian Province. It was made a town in the Tang Dynasty and a supervisory town in the Song Dynasty. In the Yuan and Ming Dynasties, the Inspection Department was established there, and in the Qing Dynasty, it served as the office of the Fuzhou Coast Defence Department. All ships in and out were subject to customs inspection there.

⊙ Min'an Inspection Department *Yamen*

Ryukyu-kan in Fuzhou, located on Guanhou Street, Taijiang District, Fuzhou City, was founded in the early Ming Dynasty. It was a garden-style hotel. As time went by, it became smaller and smaller. After the Ryukyu Kingdom abolished the Han system, Ryukyu-kan could not remain. In 1992, a 600-square-meter building was built and opened to the public as a place to promote the friendly exchanges between Fujian and Okinawa and to show the history of Fuzhou's foreign relations.

◉ Ryukyu-kan in Fuzhou

2 Tribute and Trade

During the Ming and Qing Dynasties, having seen China's social progress and economic prosperity, neighboring countries admired Chinese culture and were keen to conduct economic and trade exchanges with China. Envoys from various countries came to pay tribute, and Ryukyu was no exception. It paid tribute to Imperial China twice or more every year.

a. Tribute items

During the Ming and Qing dynasties, the Ryukyu Kingdom was the poorest in East Asia, and its tributes to China were mostly local products such as sulfur, whetstones, and kelp. In order to profit from trade, the Ryukyu Kingdom used to purchase copper, pepper, and hematoxylin (derived from logwood trees and used as a stain, ink, and textile dye) from Japan and Southeast Asian countries as tributes to China.

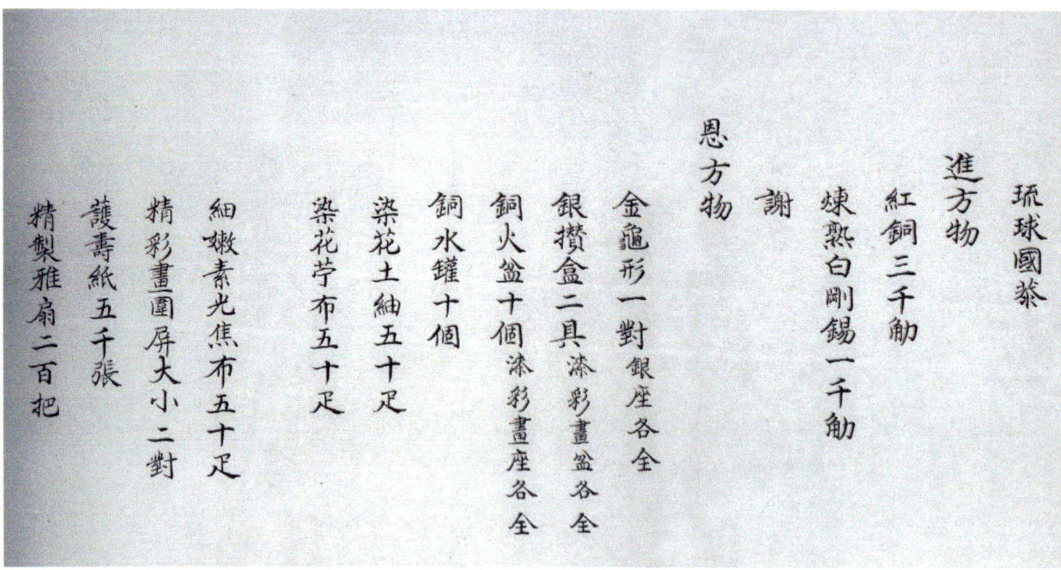
琉球國恭
進方物
紅銅三千觔
煉熟白剛錫一千觔
謝
恩方物
金龜形一對銀座各全
銀攢盒二具漆彩畫盆各全
銅火盆十個漆彩畫座各全
銅水罐十個
染花土紬五十疋
染花苧布五十疋
細嫩素光蕉布五十疋
精彩畫圍屏大小二對
護壽紙五千張
精製雅扇二百把

◉ List of tribute items from the Ryukyu Kingdom

As usual, the Chinese government would give extremely generous rewards to the overseas tributary countries, usually ten times or twenty times higher than the market price of their tributes, and bestow the envoys with clothing, money, and so on to show generosity.

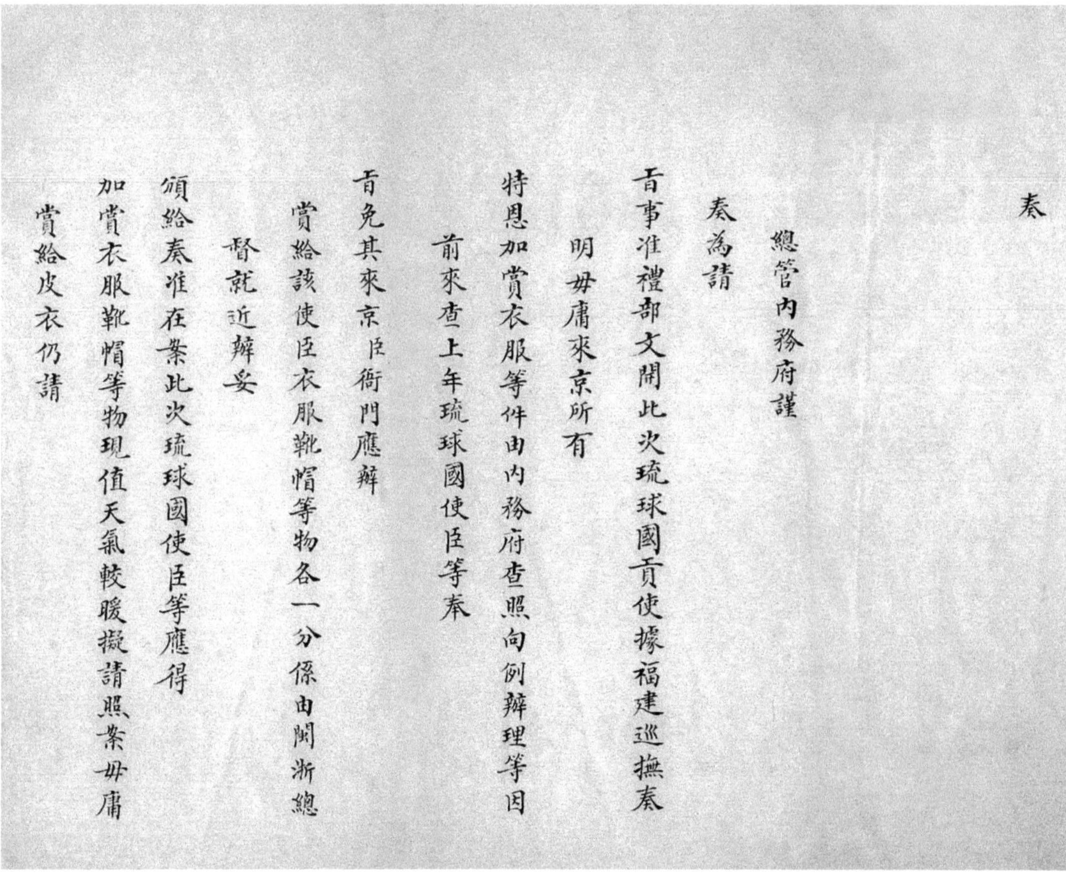

奏
總管內務府謹
奏為請
旨事准禮部文開此次琉球國貢使據福建巡撫奏
明毋庸來京所有
特恩加賞衣服等件由內務府查照向例辦理等因
前來查上年琉球國使臣等奉
旨免其來京臣衙門應辦
賞給該使臣衣服靴帽等物各一分係由閩浙總
督就近辦妥
頒給奏准在案此次琉球國使臣等應得
加賞衣服靴帽等物現值天氣較暖擬請照案毋庸
賞給皮衣仍請

⦿ Documents of the Imperial Household Department of Qing Dynasty rewarding the Ryukyu Kingdom

The craftsmanship of Ryukyu lacquerware was influenced by China and Japan. According to historical records, in 1667, Ryukyu people learned lacquerwarewas made in Fuzhou and spread it to Ryukyu. After the technique of Chinese lacquerware production was mastered by the Ryukyu people, coupled with the changes in the raw materials and ornaments of Ryukyu's first-class lacquer ware, the Ryukyu lacquerware products were favored by the rulers and ministers of the Qing Dynasty. After that, lacquerware became one of its important tribute items.

◉ Ryukyu Tribute—Large lacquer bowl

◉ Lacquer bowl

◉ Lacquer square bowl

◉ Lacquer bowl with lid

◉ Lacquer box (1)

◉ Lacquer box (2)

◉ Lacquer plate (1)

◉ Lacquer plate (2)

◉ Lacquer casket (1)

◉ Lacquer casket (2)

⊙ Lacquer screen (partial) (1)

⊙ Lacquer screen (partial) (2)

The same was true with textile craftsmanship. After the people of Ryukyu learned textile skills in Fujian in 1659 and 1736, Ryukyu's textile and handicraft industry developed rapidly. The types of textiles produced in Ryukyu have also developed from a single cloth woven from plantain fiber to silk cloth, cotton cloth, silk cloth, linen, and other materials.

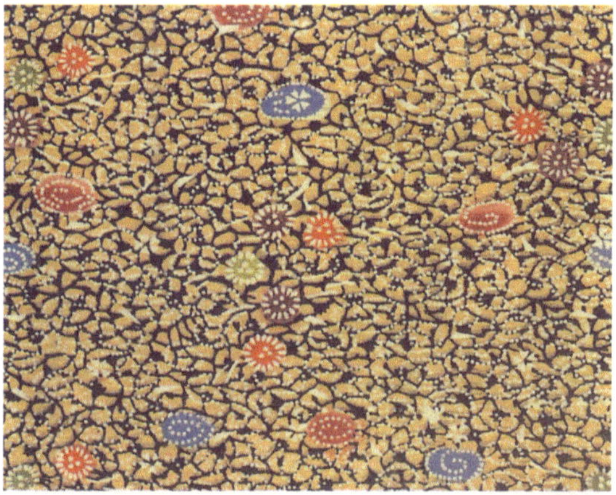

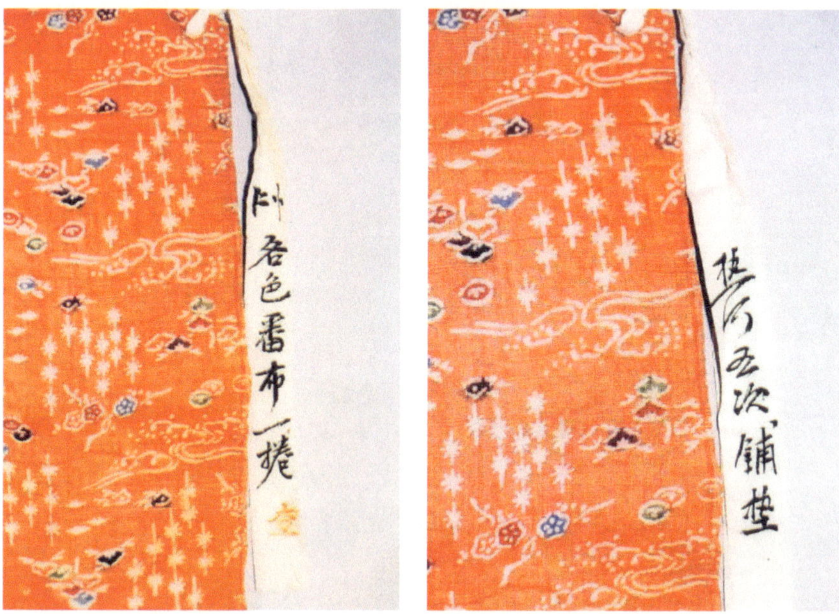

◉ Ryukyu tribute—cloth woven from plantain fiber

Most of the tributes to China from the Ryukyu Kingdom were purchased from other countries. For example, the saddles, Japanese swords, and armor that are now collected in the Forbidden City are obviously from Japan.

◉ Folding fan

◉ Harness

◉ Sword

◉ Armor

b. Trade

During the Ming and Qing Dynasties, the Ryukyu Kingdom took advantage of China's ban on maritime trade or intercourse with foreign countries, during which all trade activities between China and overseas countries almost halted, and carried out profitable intermediary trade activities. It made use of the opportunity of tributes; that is, exchanging them for a great number of Chinese goods, which it sold in Southeast Asian countries, thus earning a great profit.

The Ryukyu Kingdom used Chinese goods to engage in trade activities in overseas countries, and turned the products of overseas countries it purchased into tribute items to China.

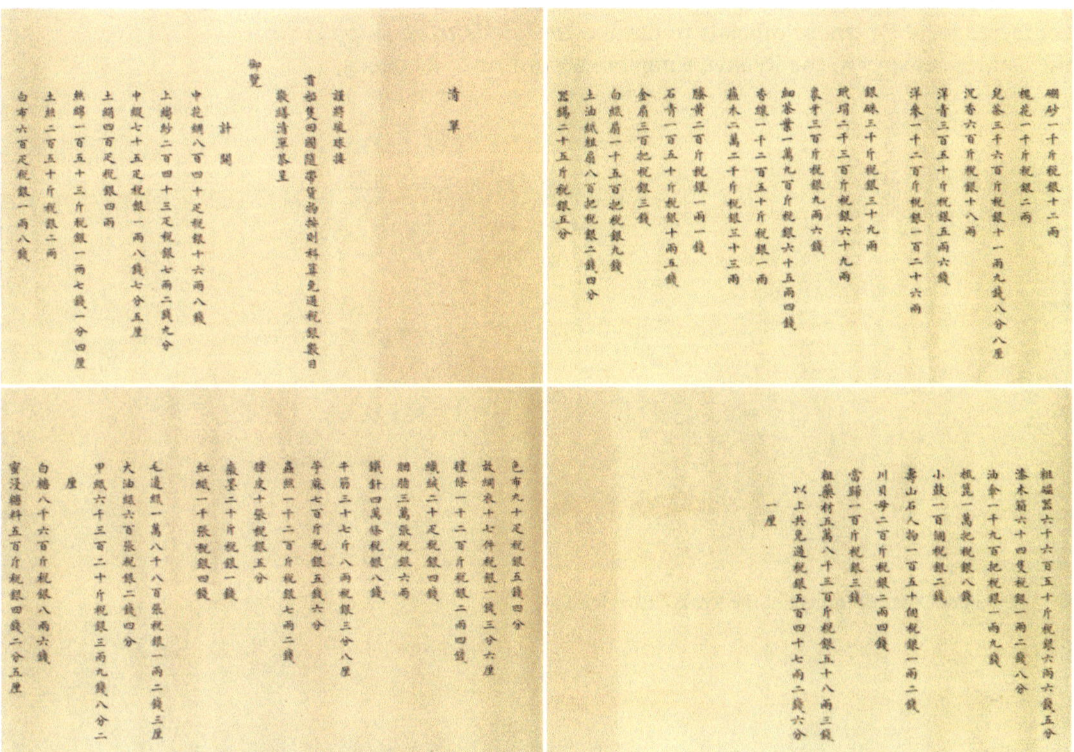

清單
護送琉球接
貢船隻回國隨帶貨物按則科算免過稅銀數目
繕具清單恭呈
御覽
計開
中花綢八百四十疋稅銀十六兩八錢
上縐紗二百四十三疋稅銀七兩二錢九分
中緞七十五疋稅銀一兩八錢七分五釐
土綢四百疋稅銀四兩
絲綿一百五十三斤稅銀一兩七錢一分四釐
土絲二百五十斤稅銀二兩
白布六百疋稅銀一兩八錢
硼砂一千斤稅銀十二兩
槐花一千斤稅銀二兩
兒茶三千六百斤稅銀十一兩九錢八分八釐
沉香六百斤稅銀十八兩
洋青三百五十斤稅銀五兩六錢
洋參一千二百斤稅銀一百二十六兩
銀硃三十斤稅銀三十九兩
玳瑁二千三百斤稅銀六十九兩
象牙三百斤稅銀九兩六錢
細茶葉一萬九百斤稅銀六十五兩四錢
香線一千二百五十斤稅銀一兩
蘇木二萬二千斤稅銀三十三兩
藤黃二百斤稅銀一兩一錢
石青一百五十斤稅銀十兩五錢
金扇三百把稅銀三錢
白紙扇一千五百把稅銀九錢
上油紙粗扇八百把稅銀二錢四分
番錫二十五斤稅銀五分
色布九十疋稅銀五錢四分
故綢衣十七件稅銀一錢三分六釐
線條一千二百斤稅銀二兩四錢
線絨二十疋稅銀四錢
綿紙三萬張稅銀六兩
鐵針四萬條稅銀八錢
牛筋三十七斤八兩稅銀三分八釐
苧麻七百斤稅銀五錢六分
蟲絲一千二百斤稅銀七兩二錢
獐皮十張稅銀五分
麁墨二十斤稅銀一錢
紅紙一千張稅銀四錢
毛邊紙一萬八千八百張稅銀一兩二錢三釐
大油紙六百張稅銀二錢四分
甲紙六千三百二十斤稅銀三兩九錢八分二
釐
白糖八千六百斤稅銀八兩六錢
蜜浸糖料五百斤稅銀四錢二分五釐
粗磁器六千六百五十斤稅銀六兩六錢五分
漆木箱六十四隻稅銀一兩二錢八分
油傘一千九百把稅銀一兩九錢
棕笠一萬把稅銀八錢
小鼓一百個稅銀二錢
壽山石人物一百五十個稅銀一兩二錢
川貝母二百斤稅銀二兩四錢
當歸一百斤稅銀三錢
粗藥材五萬八千三百斤稅銀五十八兩三錢
以上共免過稅銀五百四十七兩二錢六分
一釐

◉ List of the amount of tax-exempt silver for the goods that the ships of the Ryukyu Kingdom brought back to the country

3 Ryukyu Assessment Office and Documents

During the Ming and Qing Dynasties, the Chinese imperial mission envoys sent to Ryukyu engaged in large-scale trade. The Ryukyu institution responsible for arranging trade with the Chinese diplomatic corps was the Assessment Office, which determined the price of goods and whether the transaction would occur between China and the Ryukyu Kingdom.

Usually, the Ryukyu Assessment Office started work before the Chinese imperial mission envoys departed for the Ryukyu Kingdom. First, it checked the trades with past Chinese envoys, such as trade volume, types of goods, etc. Also, they investigated the market conditions in Fuzhou and directly contacted local Fujianese officials to discuss the goods to be shipped with the Chinese envoys to the Ryukyu Kingdom according to its needs.

◉ Assessment Office document of the Ryukyu Kingdom

4 The Ryukyu Tribute Ship

In the early years, the navigation technology of the Ryukyu Kingdom was very backward. Guided by the Fuzhou's shipbuilding technology, especially after Fujianese migrated to the Ryukyu Kingdom, its shipbuilding technology gradually developed, and historical records show that Ryukyu ships were mostly made by imitating Fuzhou *niaochuan* (literally "bird-boat" because they were shaped like birds).

⊙ Ryukyu Tribute Ship

CHAPTER 4

The Min People and the Ryukyu Kingdom

The rapid improvement of Sino-Ryukyu relations and the great progress of Ryukyu society benefited from the emigration of the 36 Min (Fujian) families to the Ryukyu Kingdom. After that, the Ryukyu Kingdom became a trade transit state.

1 Thirty-Six Families from Min

In 1392, the Emperor Taizu of Ming ordered 36 Min families to emigrate to the Ryukyu Kingdom. This was not only a special policy that the Ming Dynasty had never implemented for other overseas countries but also the only large-scale emigration overseas organized by the Chinese government. It mattered a great deal in the history of Sino-Ryukyu relations.

a. Genealogy of Min people in the Ryukyu Kingdom

Since the reform and opening up period in modern China, as economic and trade exchanges between Japan and China became more frequent, the clans of the descendants of the 36 Min families in Okinawa Prefecture of Japan regularly send members back to Fujian to seek their roots and worship their ancestors, revise their genealogy, and establish new social ties.

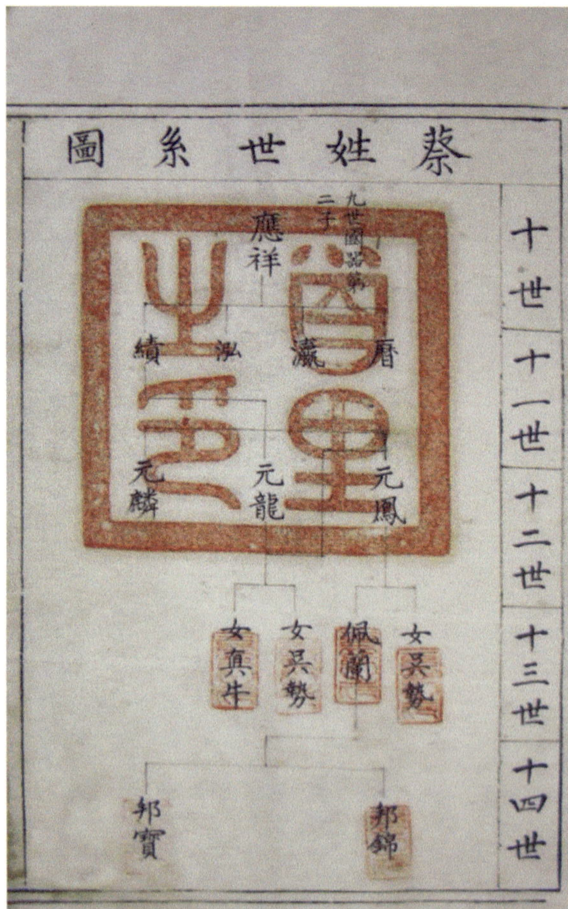

⦿ Genealogy of the Cai family

1992 is the 600th anniversary of the 36 Min families' emigration to the Ryukyu Kingdom. Japanese historians, researchers of local chronicles of Fujian, and staff from FamilySearch researched the pedigrees of the 36 Min families in Okinawa, Japan, based on documentary records and genealogy data. After several years of cooperation and effort, they have verified the ancestry of the Cai, Lin, Jin, and Liang families in Fuzhou, the Chen family in Putian, the Cai family in Quanzhou, and the Mao, Ruan, Wang, and Chen families in Zhangzhou.

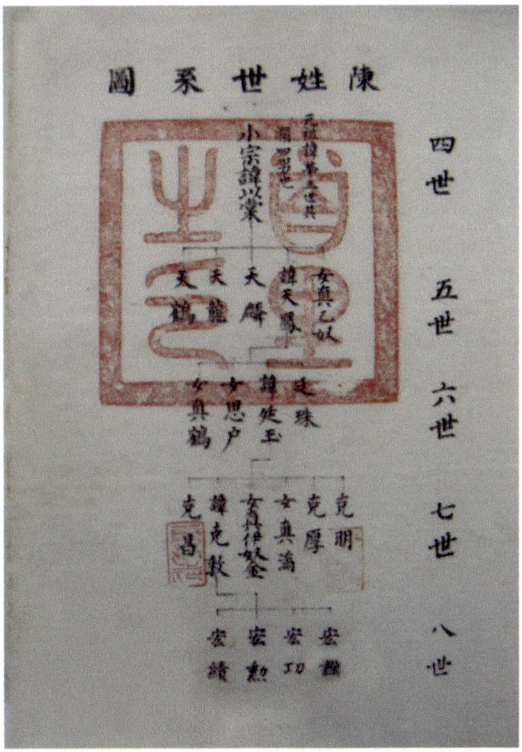

⦿ Genealogy of the Chen family

⦿ Genealogy of the Cheng family

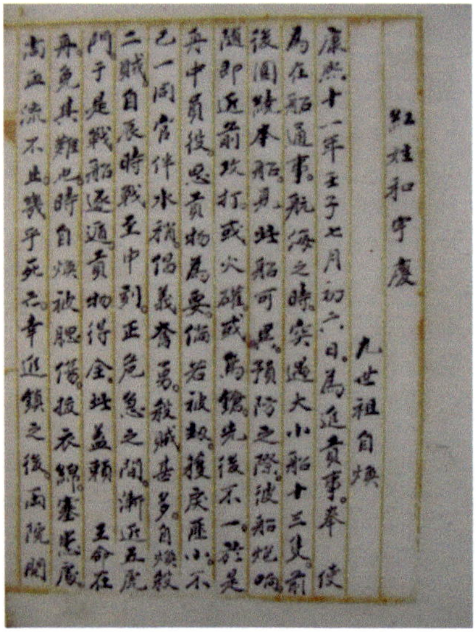

⦿ Genealogy of the Hong family

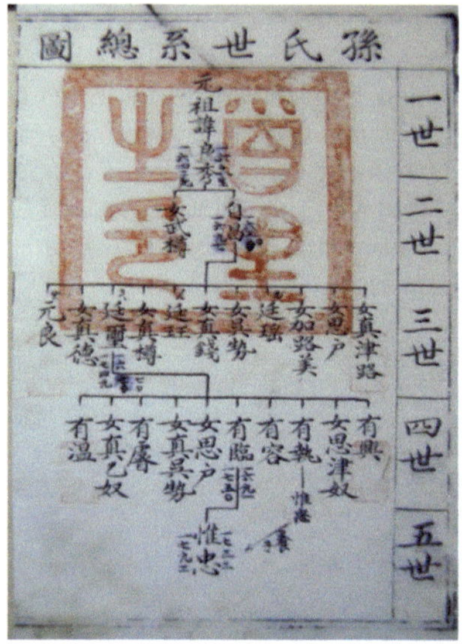

⦿ Genealogy of the Sun family

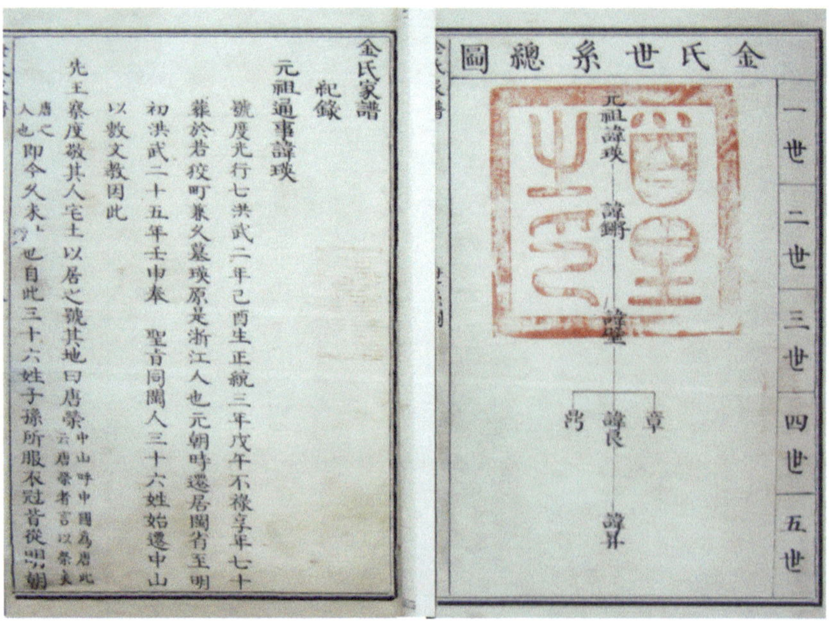

⦿ Genealogy of the Jin family

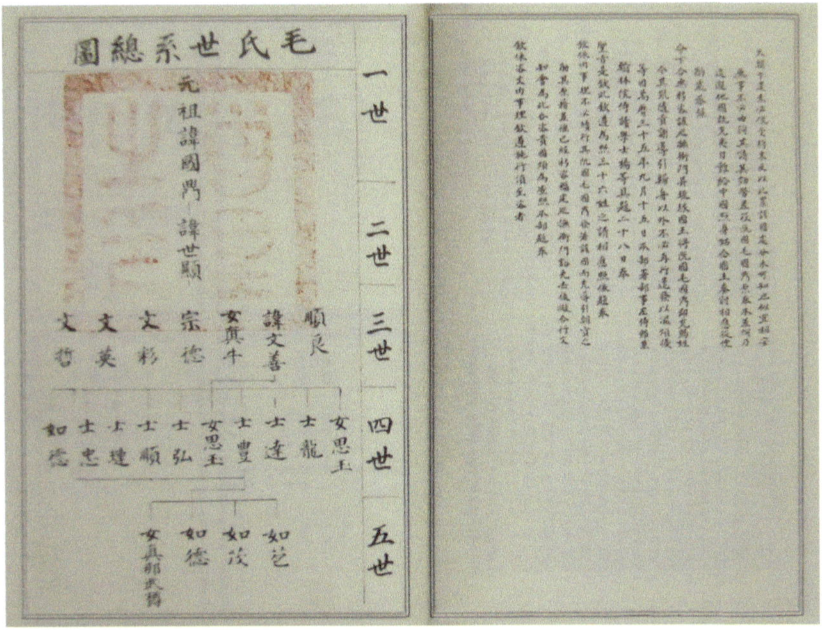

Genealogy of the Mao family

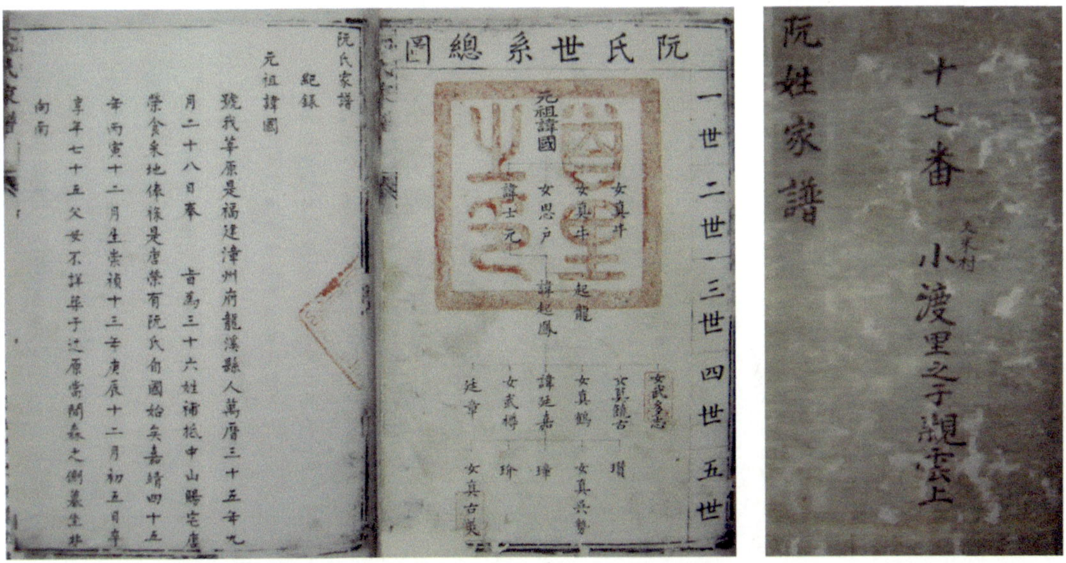

Genealogy of the Ruan family

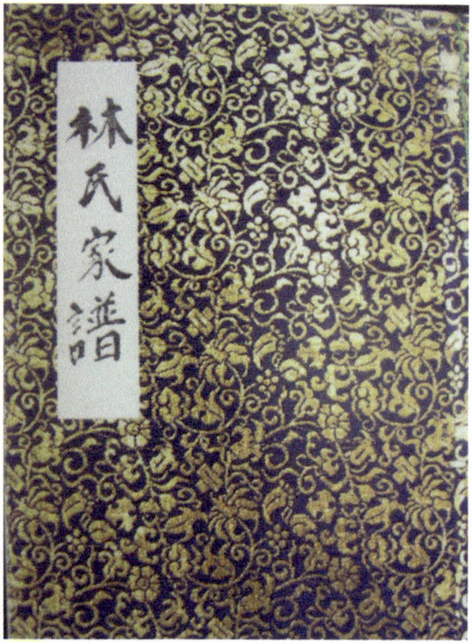

◉ Genealogy of the Lin family

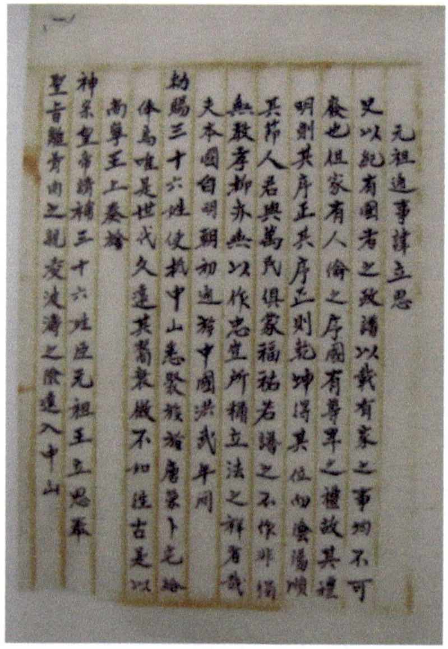

◉ Genealogy of the Wang family

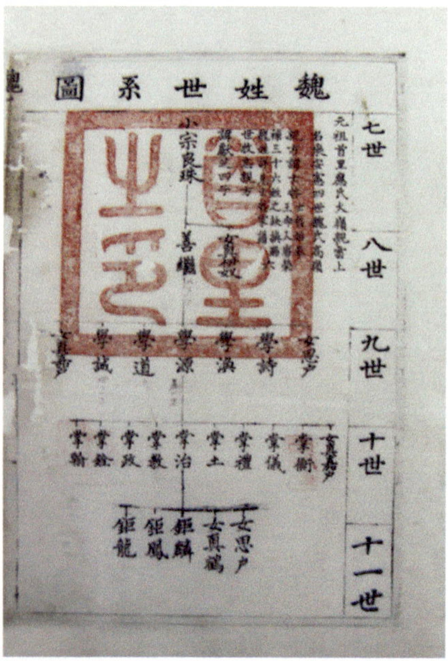

◉ Genealogy of the Wei family

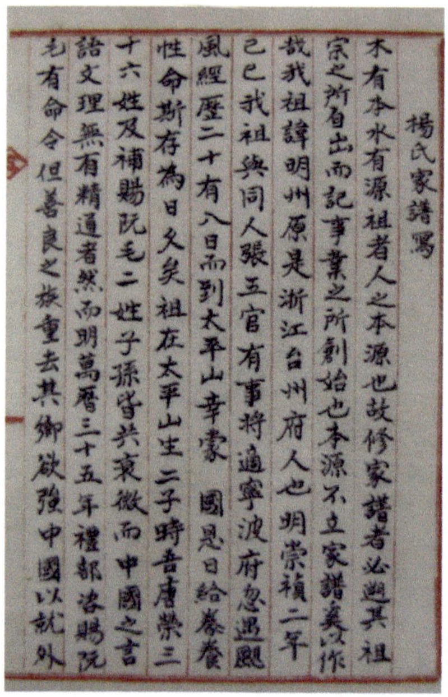

◉ Genealogy of the Yang family

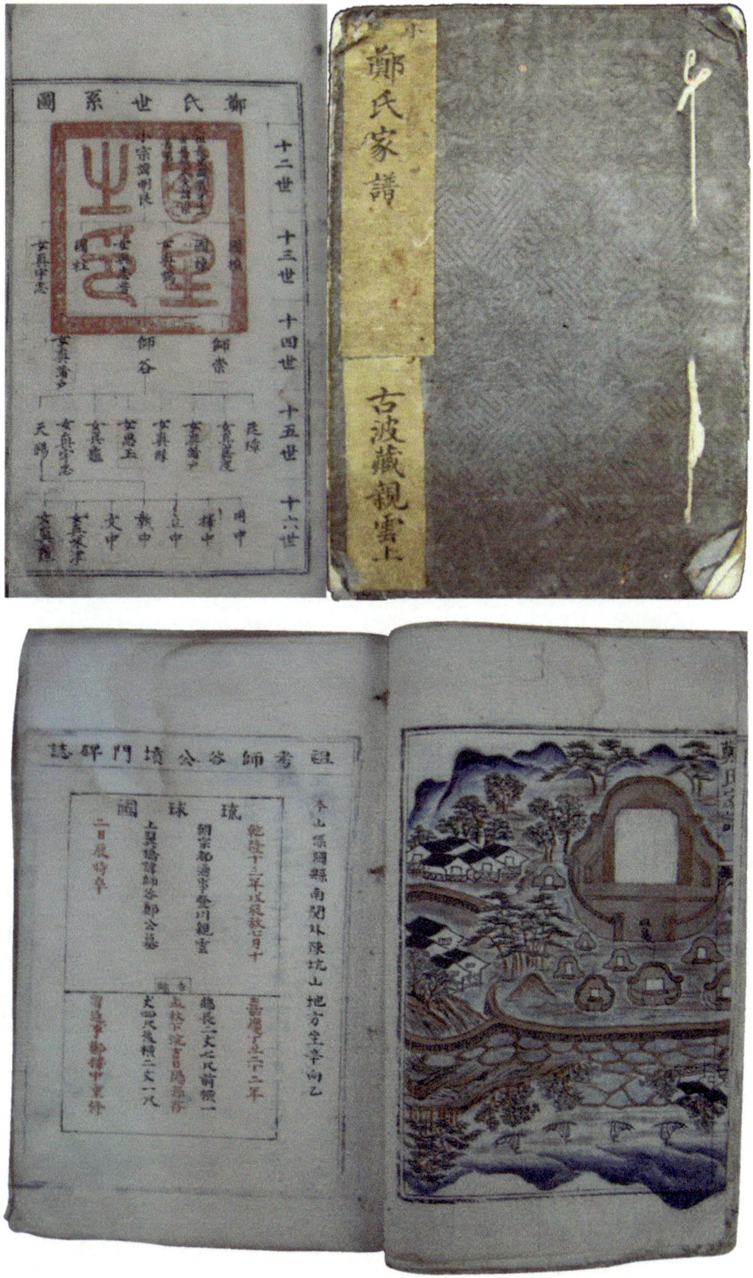

⦿ Genealogy of the Zheng family

Since then, groups of descendants of the Ryukyu Min people have embarked on a journey to find their roots in Fujian.

◉ The Ryukyu Min descendants surnamed Ruan came to Jiaomei, Zhangzhou, to worship their ancestors

◉ Liang's Ancestral Hall in Liangbian Village, Jinfeng, Changle

◉ The Ryukyu Min descendants surnamed Liang came to Changle, Fuzhou, to worship their ancestors

◉ The Ryukyu Min descendants surnamed Lin came to Linpu, Fuzhou, to worship their ancestors

b. Ryukyu Min families association

The Ryukyu Min people have gone through thick and thin. Closely linked with the fate of the Ryukyu Kingdom, they have witnessed joy and pain. They worked hard and made great contributions to the progress and prosperity of Ryukyu society. They have fully blended in, but they still remember their homeland, and the blood of their ancestors still runs through them. On December 17, 1992, the Ryukyu Min descendants held an unveiling ceremony for the monument to the birthplace of Kume Village. A stone model of a tribute ship was unveiled to the world, and all the surnames of the 36 Min families were engraved on both sides of the ship.

◉ Monument of the Birthplace of Kume Village

◉ Fujian scholars visit Liang's Wujiang Association in Okinawa

◉ Fuzhou Garden in Ryukyu

◉ White Pagoda of Fuzhou Garden in Ryukyu

2 Ryukyu Tombs and Chinese Tombs

During the exchanges between Imperial China and the Ryukyu Kingdom, all Ryukyu tribute ships and ships that carried envoys and international students had to stop in Fujian. Some of the Ryukyu people who came to China died in the storms, and some died of illness. As a result, Ryukyu tombs were built in various parts of Fujian, and there were also Chinese tombs in the Ryukyu Kingdom.

a. Ryukyu cemetery in Fuzhou

As documented, 578 Ryukyu people died in Fuzhou, most were buried where they died. In addition to the nine Ryukyu tombs in the Ryukyu cemetery, there are four Ryukyu tombs around Baiquan Nunnery, two in the Gaogai Mountains and one each in the Fujian Architecture School, Tazai Village of Shangdu, and Dinghai Town of Lianjiang. In addition, more than ten Ryukyu tombstones unearthed were collected.

◉ Ryukyu Tombs in Cangshan of Fuzhou

◉ Ryukyu Cemetery in Fuzhou

b. Chinese tombs in Ryukyu

In 1852, enslaved Chinese workers on the ship *Robert Bowne* revolted. The ship hit a rock near Yaeyama in Ryukyu. Hundreds of Chinese workers were rescued by Ryukyu locals. The British and American colonists sent warships to suppress them, causing hundreds of Chinese casualties. They were buried on Ishigaki Island of the Ryukyu Kingdom.

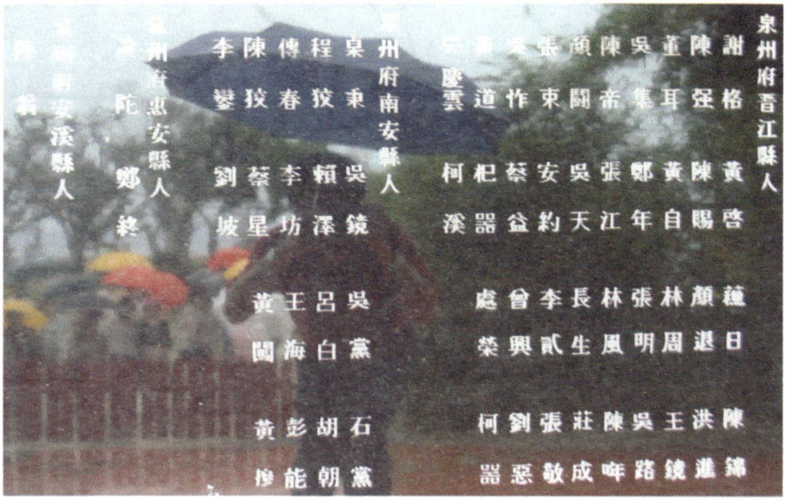

⊙ (LEFT) Chinese Tombs on Ishigaki Island

⊙ (ABOVE) Chinese tombstones on Ishigaki Island

In September 1971, the locals and the overseas Chinese on Ishigaki Island donated money to reconstruct the Chinese cemetery. Today, the tombs of the Chinese people on Ishigaki Island have become a place to pay homage to the deceased Chinese workers, a place to indict the barbaric years, a place to pray for peace, a place to mark the friendship between Japan and China, and a tourist attraction on Ishigaki Island.

⦿ Fujianese Tombstones on Ishigaki Island

CHAPTER 5

Chinese Culture in the Ryukyu Kingdom

During the Ming and Qing Dynasties, because of the maritime transportation relationship between Fujian and the Ryukyu Kingdom, the best of Chinese culture was introduced to the Ryukyu society and spread widely. It has profoundly affected all aspects of Ryukyu society, enabling it to develop and prosper.

1 Ryukyu Nobles and Commoners

Influenced by Chinese culture and political system, the Ryukyu Kingdom formed a social system with strict hierarchies where there was a great gap between nobles and commoners. And the gap was manifested in clothing, living conditions, and educational opportunities.

The Ryukyu Kingdom was deeply influenced by Fujian Province, whether in the uniforms of officials or the clothes of the common folks. In addition to the clothing of the Ryukyu king and queen, which was given directly by the Chinese government, the production of Ryukyu official uniforms and clothes shows obvious traces of the Fujian influence.

⊙ Portrait of a typical Ryukyu local

Ryukyu tribute envoys always took some Chinese clothes back to their country as examples for future tailoring. Every time the Chinese diplomatic corps departed from Fujian, tailors and craftsmen also boarded the ships, and they taught the Ryukyu people the skills of making clothes during the imperial missions.

◉ Portrait of a purple-robe Ryukyu scholar-official

⦿ Portrait of a Ryukyu monk and a Ryukyu noble

◉ Portrait of a Naha boy

◉ Portrait of a Ryukyu officer and Yaeyama People

⊙ Portrait of the Ryukyu upper class

⊙ Portrait of the Ryukyu nobles

⊙ Portraits of Ryukyu civilians and gentry

2 The Art Treasures Left by the Envoys in the Ryukyu Kingdom

In the Ming and Qing Dynasties, the imperial mission envoys, in addition to the officials stipulated by the Chinese government, also invited talents from all walks of life to sail together to the Ryukyu Kingdom. Usually, the number of people in the Chinese diplomatic corps ranged from 300 to 700. These talents communicated with all sorts of Ryukyu people, widely spread the advanced Chinese culture, and certainly impacted Ryukyu's customs, ideology, and beliefs.

The Chinese envoys sent to confer titles to the Ryukyu Kingdom in the Ming and Qing Dynasties were all well-read literati, and they left many masterpieces of calligraphy there.

Wang Ji, accredited to the Ryukyu Kingdom in 1683, left this calligraphy there.

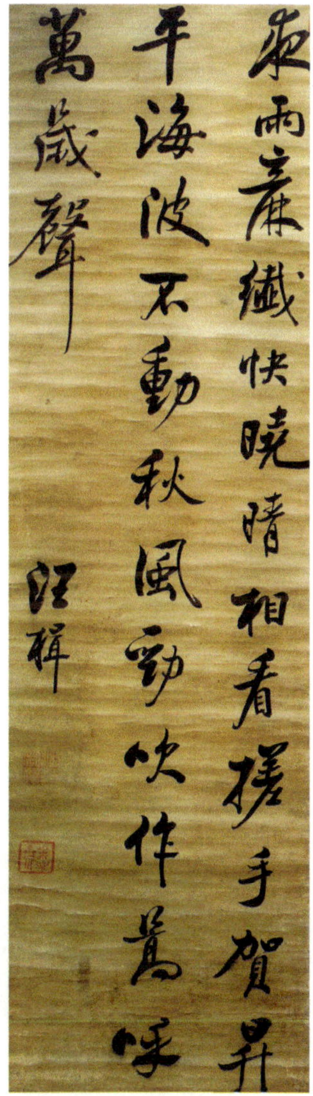

◉ Calligraphy by Wang Ji

Xu Baoguang, accredited to the Ryukyu Kingdom in 1719, wrote *Li Xue Tang* for Tei Junsoku, a learned man of the Ryukyu Kingdom.

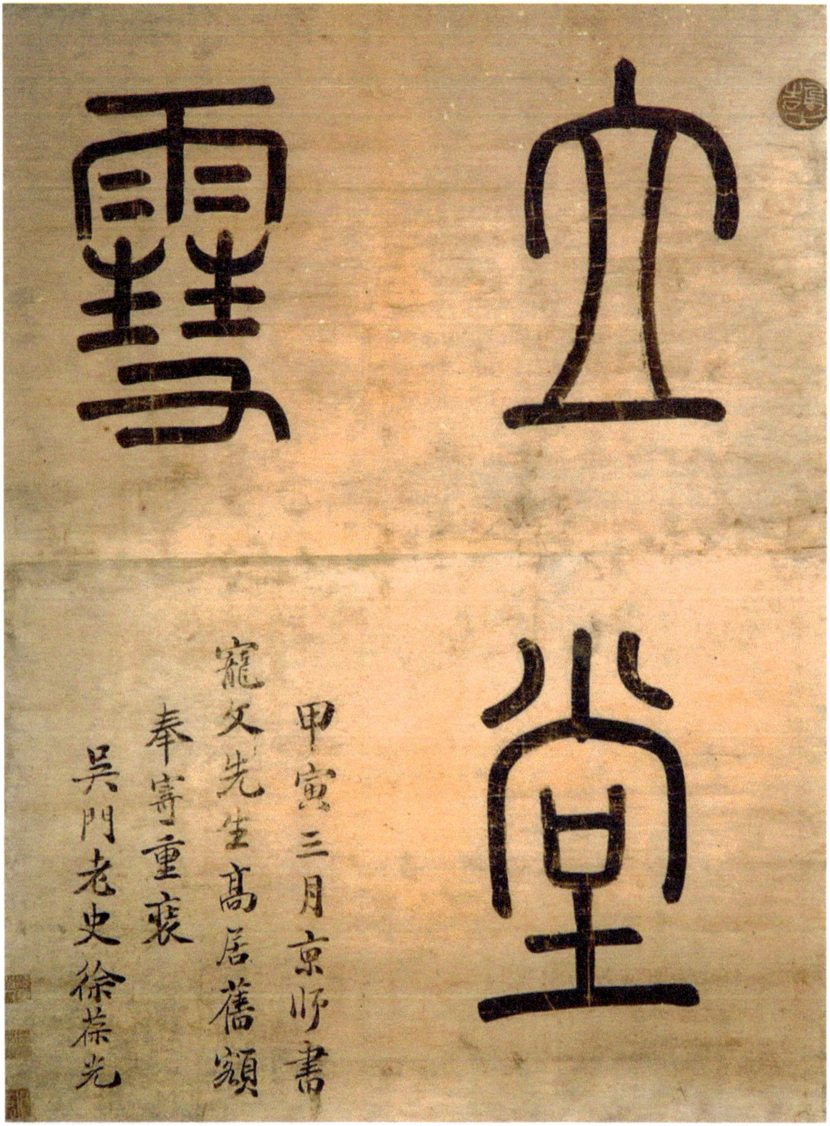

◉ *Li Xue Tang* by Xu Baoguang

Quan Kui was sent to the Ryukyu Kingdom in 1756. During his imperial mission there, he wrote a giant *fu* character for the Ryukyu people.

◉ *Fu* by Quan Kui

Wang Wenzhi (1730–1803), a native of Zhenjiang, Jiangsu Province, was a poet and calligrapher. In 1756, he went to the Ryukyu Kingdom with Quan Kui as an invited guest.

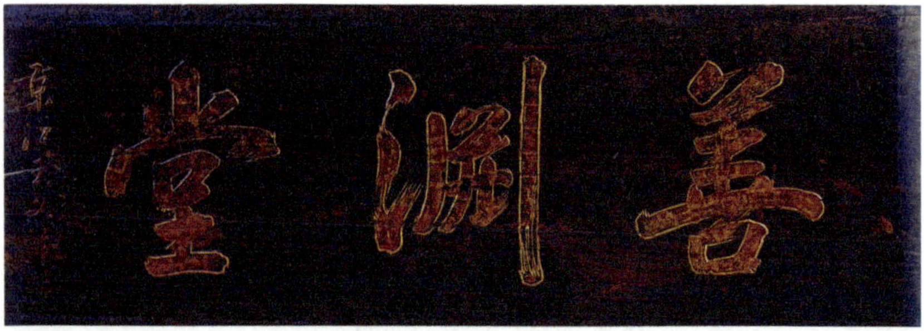

◉ The plaque inscribed by Wang Wenzhi

Ji Chen, a native of Hengshan, traveled to the Ryukyu Kingdom as an invited guest during the Jiaqing period of the Qing Dynasty (1796–1821).

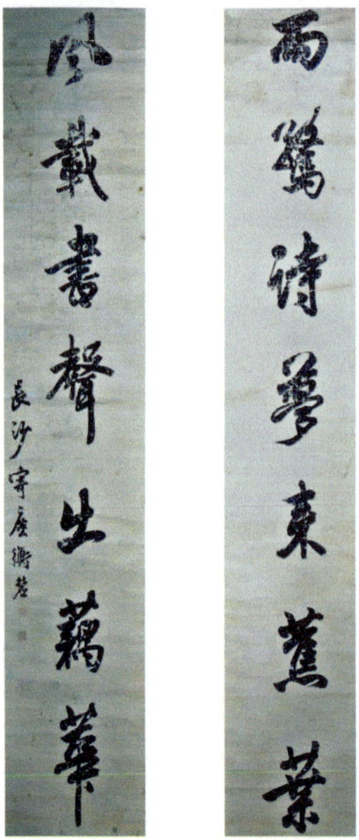

◉ Couplets inscribed by Ji Chen

Zhao Wenkai (1760–1808), a native of Taihu, Anhui Province, went to the Ryukyu Kingdom in 1800.

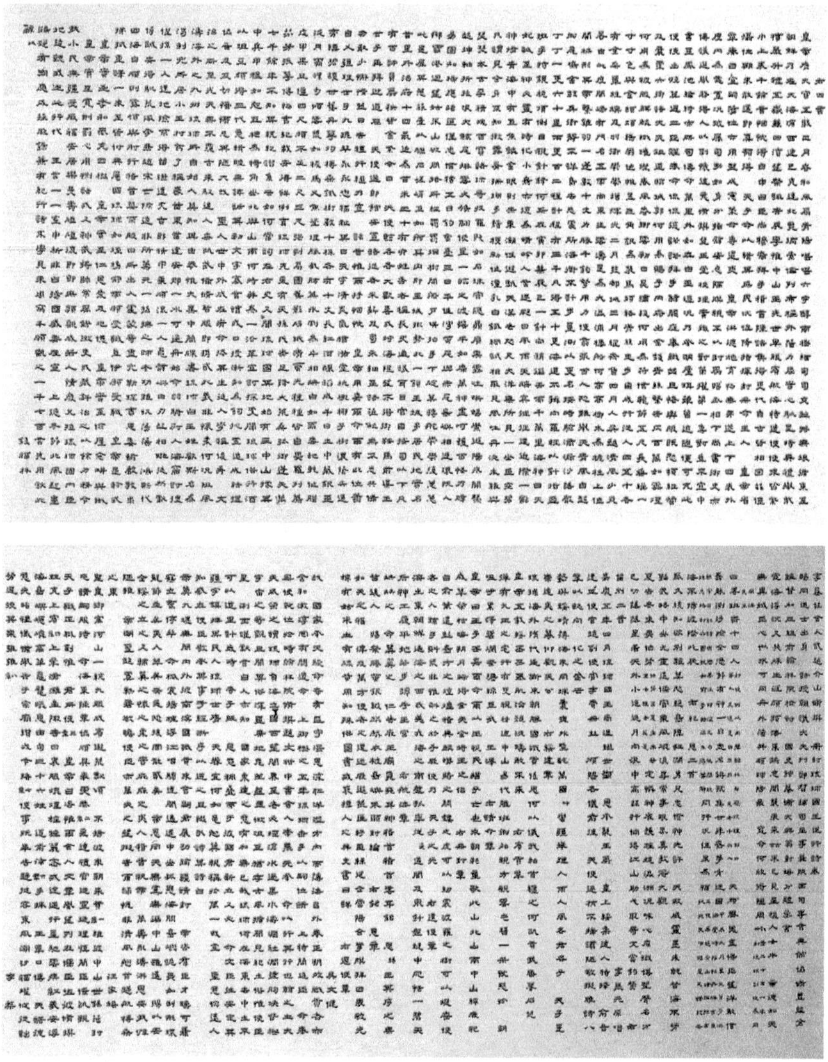

⊙ Poetry by Zhao Wenkai

Qi Kun was an envoy sent to the Ryukyu Kingdom in 1808. This piece of his calligraphy is preserved in the Okinawa Prefectural Museum of Japan.

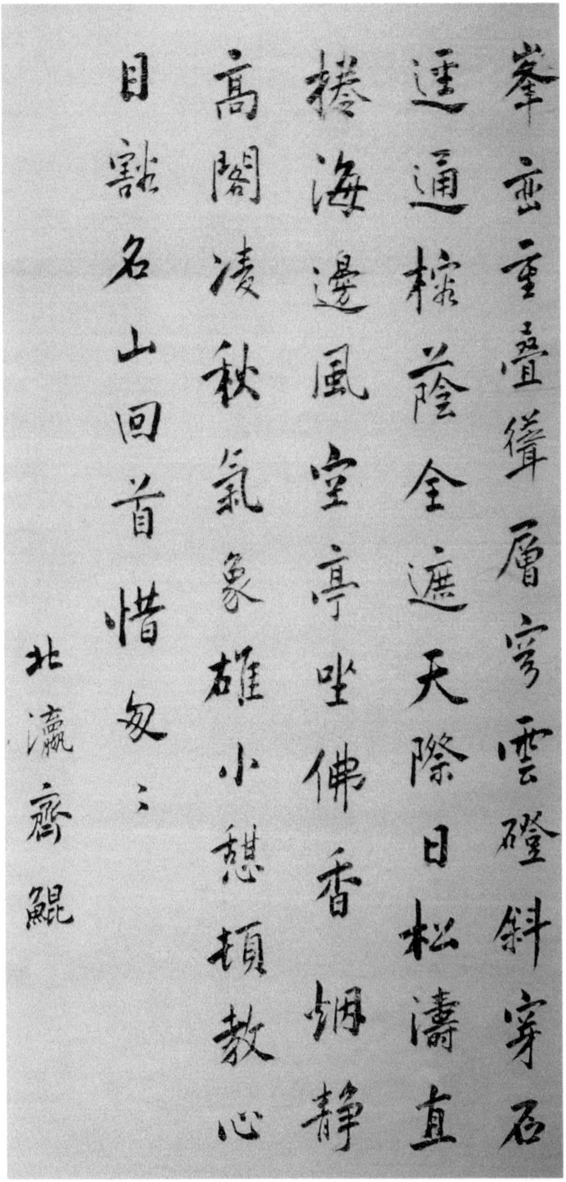

Calligraphy by Qi Kun during his imperial mission in the Ryukyu Kingdom

Lin Hongnian (1804–1886), a native of Fuzhou, Fujian Province, was sent to the Ryukyu Kingdom as an envoy in 1838.

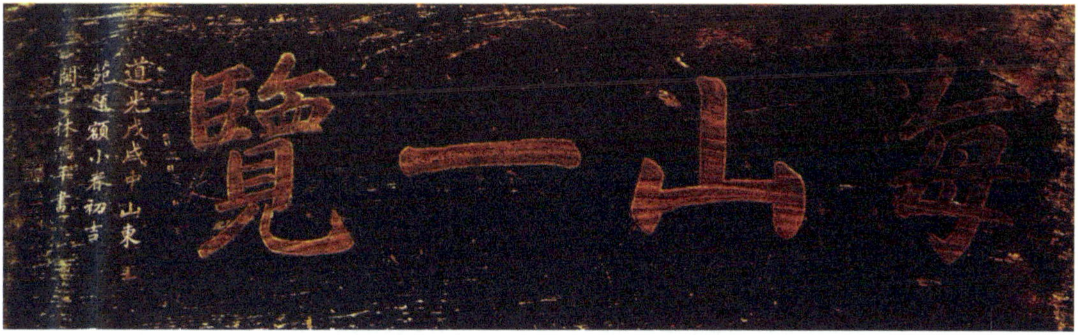

⦿ The plaque inscribed by Lin Hongnian: *Hai Shan Yi Lan*

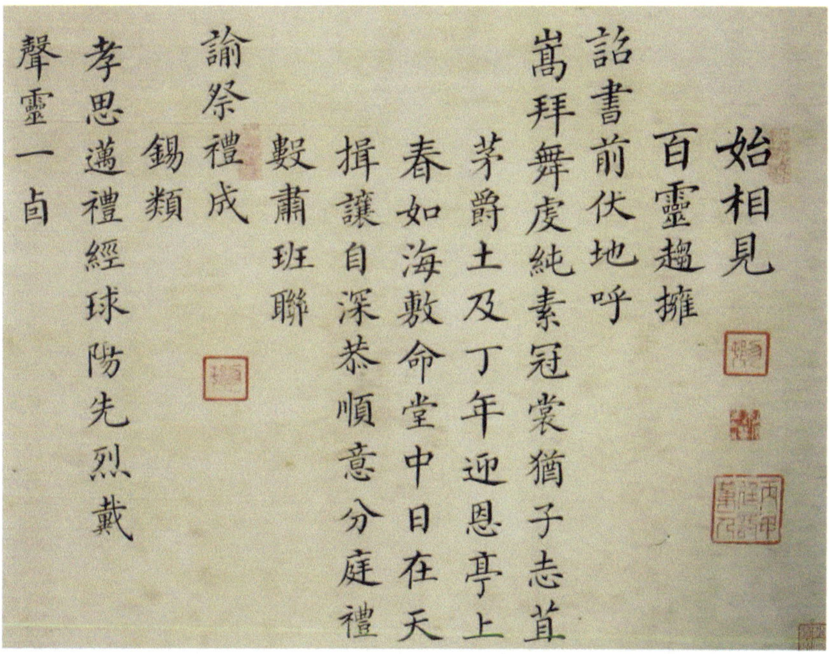
始相見
百靈趨擁
詔書前伏地呼
嵩拜舞虔純素冠裳猶子志萓
茅爵土及丁年迎恩亭上
春如海敷命堂中日在天
揖讓自深恭順意分庭禮
轂肅班聯
諭祭禮成
錫類
孝思邁禮經球陽先烈戴
聲靈一卣

⦿ The book Lin Hongnian presented to the King of the Ryukyu Kingdom

Zhao Xin (1809–1876), a native of Fuzhou, was the last Chinese envoy to the Ryukyu Kingdom.

Yu Guangjia (1822–1871) accompanied Zhao Xin to the Ryukyu Kingdom in 1866.

⦿ Couplets inscribed by Zhao Xin

⦿ Couplets inscribed by Yu Guangjia

3 Fujian Cuisine and Ryukyu Cuisine

Fujian cuisine and Ryukyu cuisine are inextricably linked. In the 1990s, many Okinawan scholars came to Fuzhou to explore the connection between Fujian cuisine and Ryukyu cuisine.

How Fujian cuisine was in the Ming and Qing Dynasties is not documented, but a bite of Ryukyu cuisine can answer this question. Through the Chinese envoys sent to the Ryukyu Kingdom, the Ryukyu tribute envoys sent to Fujian, the Fujianese who emigrated to the Ryukyu Kingdom, and the Ryukyu students who studied in Fujian, Ryukyu cuisine has combined the taste, the look, and the features of Fujian cuisine in the Ming and Qing dynasties, and been passed down to the present day.

⊙ Ryukyu cuisine under the influence of Fujian cuisine—stewed trotters (pig's feet) with kelp

◉ Braised pork in brown sauce

◉ Fried pork with towel gourd

◉ Fried tofu with bean sprouts

◉ Fried pork with pickled cabbage

◉ Fried bitter gourd

◉ Red rice cake

◉ Pickled leek

◉ Ryukyu pastry under the influence of Fujian cuisine—rice cake

◉ Ryukyu brown sugar

◉ Almond cookie

4 Ryukyu International Students and Chinese Culture

Ryukyu sent over 20 batches of international students to Imperial China, which are called *guansheng* (official students) in Ming and Qing historical documents. In addition to *guansheng*, there were quite many Ryukyu people coming to study in Ryukyu-kan in Fuzhou, learning professional knowledge and production technology. Historically, Ryukyu students studying in Fuzhou were called *qinxue* (diligent students).

a. Ryukyu *guansheng* from the Imperial College

For Ryukyu students to study in China, the King of the Ryukyu Kingdom had first to petition the Chinese government. After receiving approval from the Chinese government, the Ryukyu students would board a tribute ship, land in Fuzhou, travel thousands of miles, and enroll in the Imperial College in Beijing to study.

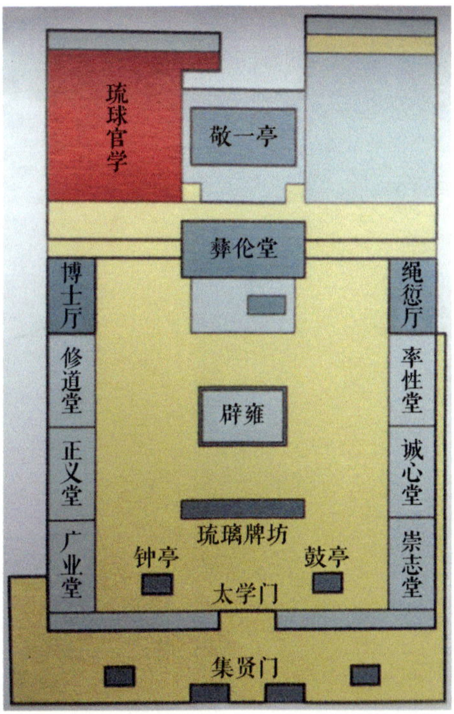

◉Schematic diagram of the Ryukyu School of Imperial College

After the Ryukyu students arrived in China, the officials of the Imperial College interviewed them, tested their Chinese proficiency, and asked them about their goals and interests in studying. At the same time, the Imperial College, as usual, selected students with excellent knowledge and good conduct as *jiaoxi* (a title for a teacher/exam manager for Chinese scholars). Next, Ryukyu students entered the lecture hall to study.

⦿ Beijing Imperial College Street, where the Ryukyu School was located

⦿ The glazed gate in the Imperial College

Ryukyu students had to complete a four-year study in China. Those who completed their studies and returned to the Ryukyu Kingdom were usually highly valued by the Ryukyu king. And they played a vital role in spreading Chinese culture, governing their country, and strengthening the friendly relations between China and the Ryukyu Kingdom.

b. Tei Junsoku, a Ryukyu Confucian scholar

In 1683, Tei Junsoku, a Ryukyu native, came to study abroad in Ryukyu-kan in Fuzhou. He devoted himself to studying Confucian classics for four years. And the four-year study and life abroad deepened his understanding of Chinese culture and laid the foundation for spreading Chinese culture in the Ryukyu Kingdom in the future, governing the Ryukyu Kingdom, and promoting the friendly development of Sino-Ryukyu relations.

In 1687, Tei Junsoku returned to the Ryukyu Kingdom after completing his studies, and was highly regarded by the Ryukyu government. He became a lecturer specializing in Confucianism. He also founded a school in the Ryukyu Kingdom to develop education in the country.

◉ Portrait of Tei Junsoku

In 1689, Tei Junsoku traveled to China again for official business. During a three-year stay in Fuzhou, he not only became more proficient in Confucianism but also purchased seventeen Chinese history classics and donated them to the Confucian Temple in the Ryukyu Kingdom after returning home.

◉ Confucian Temple in the Ryukyu Kingdom

In 1696, Tei Junsoku came to China to pay tribute to the emperor, and when he was in Fuzhou, he published the *Chūzan Poetry Collection*. He also sorted out over 80 Chinese poems he wrote, compiled them into an anthology of poems called *Xue Tang Yan You Cao,* and published it, making it a representative of Chinese poetry in the Ryukyu Kingdom.

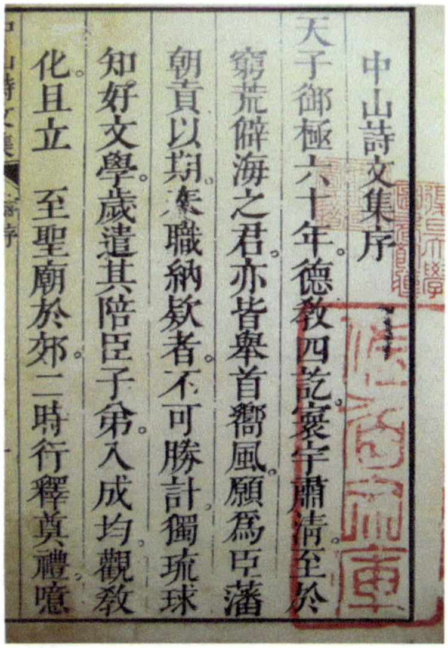

中山詩文集序
天子御極六十年德教四訖寰宇肅清至於
窮荒僻海之君亦皆舉首嚮風願爲臣藩
朝貢以[illegible]奉職納欵者不可勝計獨琉球
知好文學歲遣其陪臣子弟入成均觀教
化且立 至聖廟於郊二時行釋奠禮噫

⊙ *Chūzan Poetry Collection* by Tei Junsoku, 1721 edition, sample page

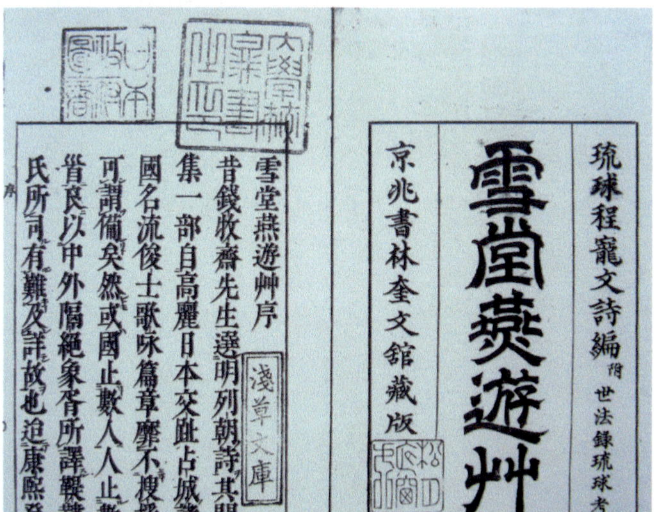

琉球程寵文詩編 附 世法録琉球考
雪堂燕遊艸
京兆書林奎文舘藏版

雪堂燕遊艸序
昔錢牧齋先生選明列朝詩其閏
集一部自高麗日本交趾占城諸
國名流俊士歌咏篇章靡不搜採
可謂備矣然或國止數人人止數
首良以中外隔絕象胥所譯鞮鞻
氏所司有難及詳故也迨康熙癸

⊙ *Xue Tang Yan You Cao* by Tei Junsoku, 1714, Kuiwenguan edition, sample page

In 1706, after Tei Junsoku went to Beijing to pay tribute to the imperial court, he returned to Fuzhou with the Ryukyu envoys to wait for a ship to return to the Ryukyu Kingdom. During his short stay in Fuzhou, he also paid to print a copy of both *Liu Yu Yan Yi* (*Explanation of Six Aspects*) and *Zhi Nan Guang Yi* (*Navigation Guide Book*) and brought them back to the Ryukyu Kingdom.

Liu Yu Yan Yi is a Confucian book written by Chinese scholar Fan Hong. It had a great impact on Ryukyu Confucianism and even became a textbook for Ryukyu people to learn Chinese.

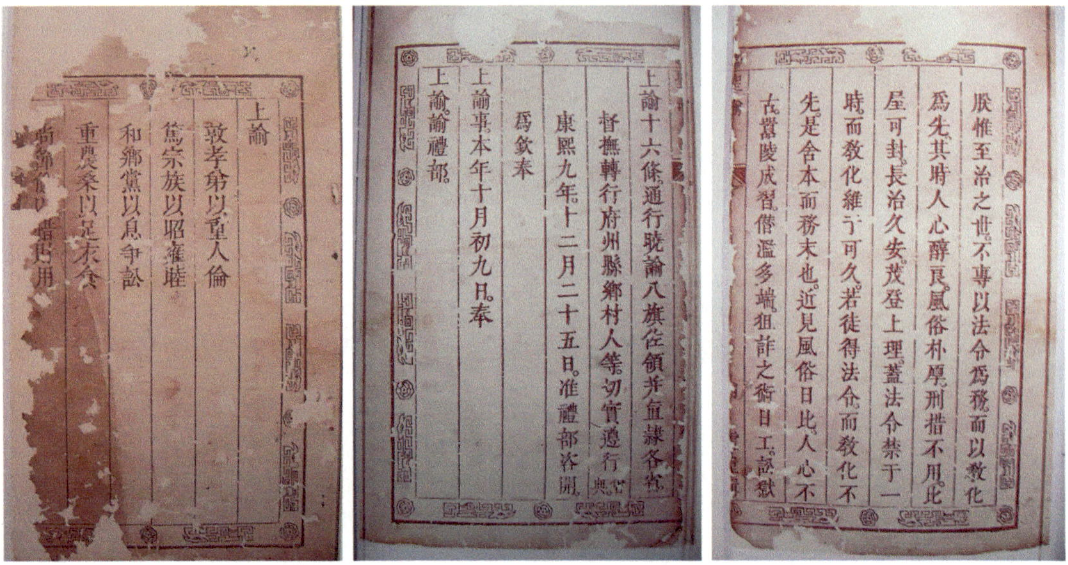

上諭
敦孝弟以重人倫
篤宗族以昭雍睦
和鄉黨以息爭訟
重農桑以足衣食
尚節儉以惜財用

上諭十六條通行曉諭八旗佐領并直隸各省
督撫轉行府州縣鄉村人等切實遵行欽此
康熙九年十二月二十五日准禮部咨開
為欽奉
上諭事本年十月初九日奉
上諭諭禮部

朕惟至治之世不專以法令為務而以教化
為先其時人心醇良風俗朴厚刑措不用比
屋可封長治久安茂登上理蓋法令禁于一
時而教化維于可久若徒恃法令而教化不
先是舍本而務末也近見風俗日敝人心不
古囂陵成習僭濫多端狙詐之術日工訟獄

⦿ *Liu Yu Yan Yi* that Tei Junsoku had ordered in Fuzhou in 1708, sample page

5 Ryukyu Garden Architecture and Burial Customs

Because of the close communication between Fujian and the Ryukyu Kingdom, Fujian's garden architectural style and burial customs were absorbed by the Ryukyu Kingdom.

According to the records of Ryukyu historical documents, in the Shō Shin era (1477–1527), the Fujianese who emigrated to the Ryukyu Kingdom led the construction of Yuanjue Temple for the Ryukyu royal family. The stone bridge over the pond of freeing captive animals in the temple completely retains the bridge building style of the Fujianese who migrated to the Ryukyu Kingdom.

Because the Fujianese who emigrated to the Ryukyu Kingdom and many Ryukyu people were buried in Fuzhou after their deaths, the construction technology and style of Fuzhou tombs were also passed on to the Ryukyu Kingdom intact, so many tortoiseshell tombs were popular in southern China preserved in the Ryukyu Kingdom.

⦿ Tortoiseshell tomb in the Ryukyu Kingdom

6 Fujian Religious Customs in the Ryukyu Kingdom

The exchanges between Fujian and the Ryukyu Kingdom introduced Buddhism, Taoism, Shamanism, and other folk religions into the Ryukyu Kingdom through various channels.

The most significant influence of Fujian on Ryukyu religious beliefs is the understanding and application of *fengshui*. The Ryukyu king sent people to Fujian in 1667, 1708, and 1848 to learn *fengshui* and implement it in the Ryukyu Kingdom. *Fengshui* was applied in the construction of temples, royal tombs, palaces, and villages in the Ryukyu Kingdom, as well as the planting of trees in mountains and forests.

Other religious beliefs in Ryukyu, such as the kitchen god, the god of land, the worship of Emperor Guan, the stone lions that exorcise ghosts and ward off evil spirits, and the application of Taishan shigandang, were brought back by Ryukyu students and Ryukyu people living in Fuzhou.

⦿ Folk beliefs of the Ryukyu Kingdom

◉ Ritual site in Nakijin Castle in the Ryukyu Kingdom

◉ Belief in the God of Land in the Ryukyu Kingdom

⦿ (LEFT) Belief in Fulu (Daoist incantations and magic symbols) in the Ryukyu Kingdom

⦿ (ABOVE) Portrait of Emperor Guan in the Ryukyu Kingdom

⦿ Stone lions in the Ryukyu Kingdom

◉ Portrait of the Ryukyu God of Fu (fortune), Lu (prosperity), and Shou (longevity)

(LEFT) Shigandang in the Ryukyu Kingdom

(BELOW) Dragon King Temple plaque in the Ryukyu Kingdom

7 Chinese Poetry and Chinese Language in the Ryukyu Kingdom

The influence of Fujian culture on Ryukyu literature and art is obvious in many aspects, and Ryukyu Chinese poetry is one of them. Most of the poets of Ryukyu Chinese poems have studied and lived in Fujian, their knowledge came from Fujian, and their poems wrote about situations in Fujian. *Ryukyu Poetry Lessons* and *Ryukyu Poetry Collection* are both excellent examples.

In 1844, Sun Yiyan, a Ryukyu *jiaoxi* at the Imperial College, selected the poems by Ryukyu student Ruan Xuanzhao and others during their studies, made comments, and published them as *Ryukyu Poems Collection*. Later, Xu Gan, a teacher, also compiled the poems of Ryukyu students Lin Shigong and others into a book and published it as *Ryukyu Poetry Lessons*.

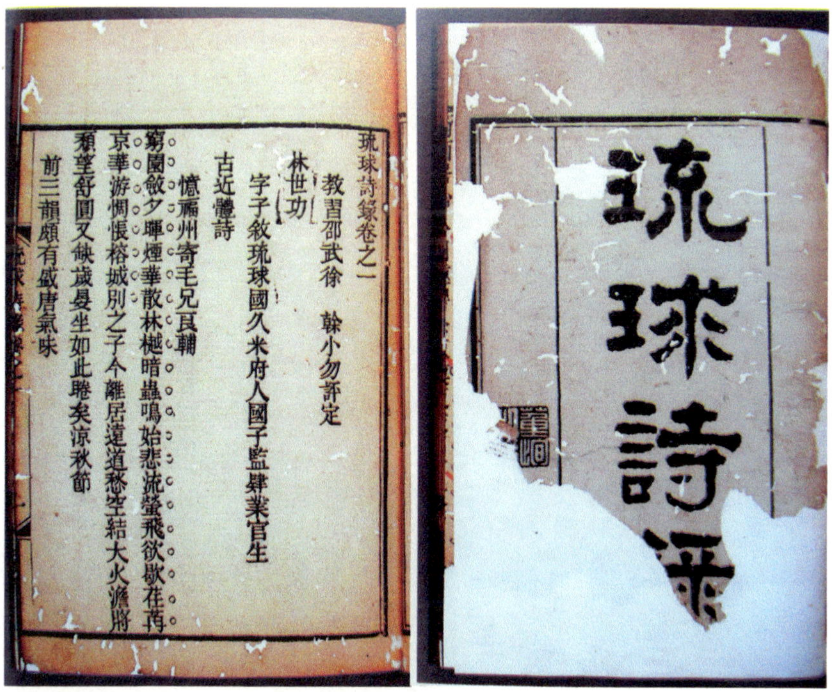
琉球詩錄卷之一
教習邵武徐　幹小勿評定
林世功
字子敘琉球國久米府人國子監肄業官生
古近體詩
憶福州寄毛兄艮輔
窮園斂夕暉煙華散林樾暗蟲鳴始悲流螢飛欲歇荏苒
京華游惆悵榕城別之子今離居遑道愁空結大火瀉將
頹望舒圓又缺歲晏坐如此睠矣涼秋節
前三韻頗有盛唐氣味

琉球詩

⦿ *Ryukyu Poetry Collection*, sample page

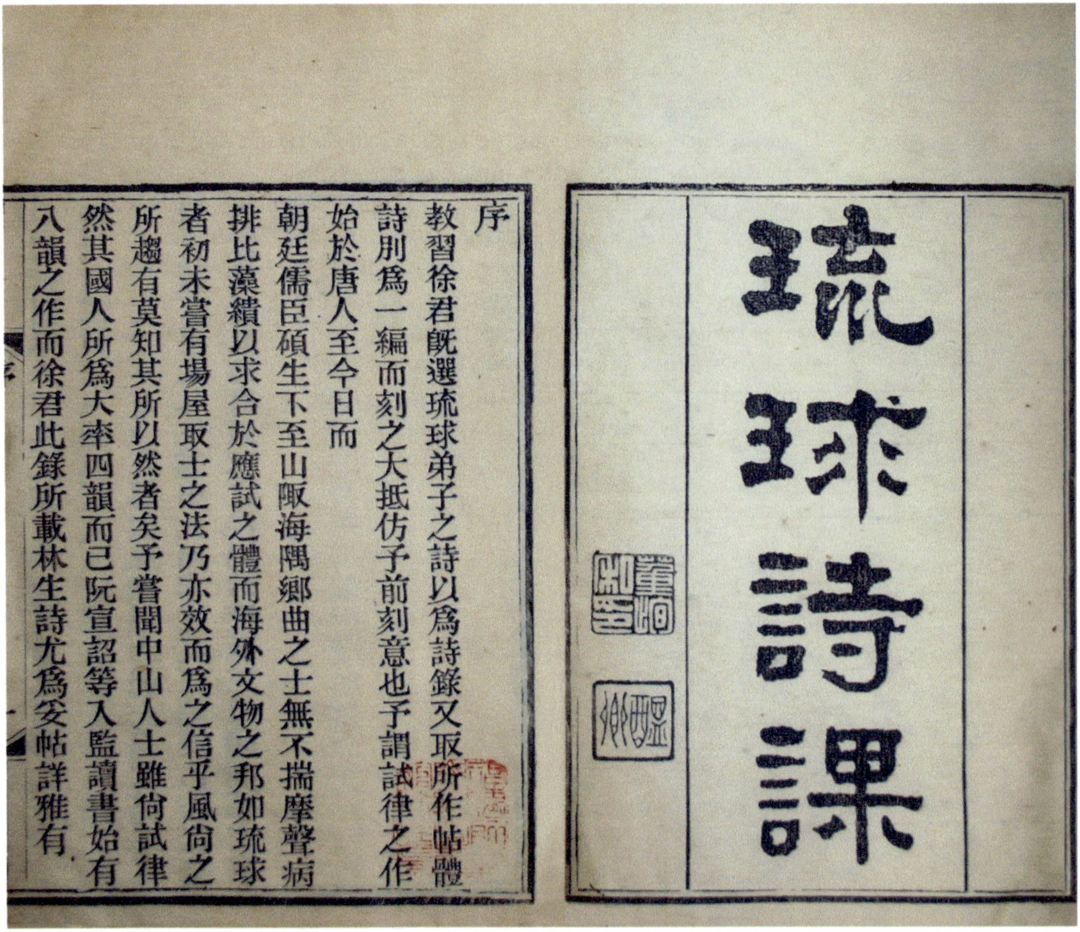

琉球詩課

序

教習徐君旣選琉球弟子之詩以爲詩錄又取所作帖體
詩別爲一編而刻之大抵仿予前刻意也予謂試律之作
始於唐人至今日而
朝廷儒臣碩生下至山陬海隅鄉曲之士無不揣摩聲病
排比藻繢以求合於應試之體而海外文物之邦如琉球
者初未嘗有場屋取士之法乃亦效而爲之信乎風尚之
所趨有莫知其所以然者矣予嘗聞中山人士雖尙試律
然其國人所爲大率四韻而已阮宣詔等入監讀書始有
八韻之作而徐君此錄所載林生詩尤爲妥帖詳雅有

◉ *Ryukyu Poetry Lesson*, sample page

In the long-term exchanges between Fujian and the Ryukyu Kingdom, it was common for Ryukyu people to learn Chinese. Today, there are still many words in the Ryukyu dialect that have the same pronunciation as the Fujian dialect, such as cat, pig, pumpkin, and more. In the Ryukyu Kingdom, there are various readers for learning Chinese, such as official mandarin language readers and common Mandarin language readers. Even its primary language was Chinese.

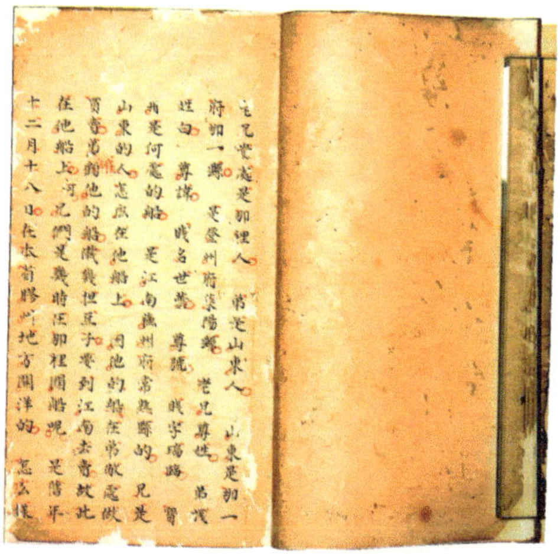

◉ (LEFT) *Official Mandarin Language Reader*, sample page

◉ (BELOW) *Ryukyu Dialect*, sample page

Summary

The research on the historical relationship between China and the Ryukyu Kingdom involves a wide range of aspects. From the 36 Min families that emigrated to the Ryukyu Kingdom, we can discuss the emigration policy in Chinese history. From the positions and roles of the 36 Min families in the Ryukyu Kingdom, we can discuss the historical evolution of overseas Chinese. From the Ming and Qing Dynasties. The Ryukyu Kingdom sent many international students to study in China, so there is the system of training and managing foreign students in ancient China to be studied. From studying the historical relationship between the two ancient countries, we can understand the selection system, reward and punishment system, and a series of strict regulations for Chinese envoys to visit foreign land in ancient times.

The history of maritime exchanges between Fujian and the Ryukyu Kingdom allows us to see the formation, development, and prosperity of the Fujian-Ryukyu Maritime Silk Road more clearly. Simply put, the sea is not a moat or a barrier, but a link, a bridge, and a channel for China to communicate with other countries in the world. In the 21st century, we need to build a new Maritime Silk Road to connect the world through the sea. We should draw nourishment from the ancient Maritime Silk Road, revive the maritime glory, and create a victorious future.

References

Fang, Baochuan, and Xie Bizhen. *Compilation of Ryukyu Documents and Historical Materials.* Ocean Publishing House, 2014.

The First Historical Archives of China. *Selected Archives of Sino-Ryukyu Relations in the Qing Dynasty*. Zhonghua Book Company, 1993.

Huang, Runhua, and Xue Ying. *Compilation of Ryukyu Materials from the National Library of China*. Beijing Library Press, 2003.

National Palace Museum, Taipei. *Compilation of Ryukyu Historical Materials in the Qing Dynasty*. 2015.

———. *Pictures about Parade of Vassals*. 2015.

Niijima, Masako. *My Ryukyu Cuisine*. Japan: Shibata Bookstore, 1989.

Okinawa Prefectural Museum, Japan. *Restore the Glory of the Ryukyu Kingdom.* 2008.

Shun Feng Xiang Song. Baudlin Library, Oxford University, UK, photocopy.

Uehara, Masahiro et al. *The Great Ryukyu in Blue Eye.* New Japan Educational Books Co., Ltd., 1987.

Yu Xia Ji Tong Shu Guang Ji. Fu Sheng Yi Wen Tang, the Eighth Year of Guangxu (1782).

About the Chief Editor

Mr. Xie Bizhen, Professor and Doctoral Supervisor of Fujian Normal University, Director of the Fujian-Taiwan Regional Research Center of Fujian Normal University, a key research base of humanities and social sciences of the Ministry of Education. His main research focuses on Chinese overseas transportation and trade history, the history of Sino-Japanese relations, and the local history of Fujian.

About the Authors

Xie Chen is a librarian and assistant researcher at the Fujian Normal University Center for Fujian-Ryukyu Relations. He received his master's degree in literature from Fujian Normal University in 2013, after studying at the University of the Ryukyus in Japan. Xie's research interests include the history of Fujian-Ryukyu relations and Fujian-Taiwan relations.

Lin Yanxi is a teacher at the School of Architecture and Urban Planning at Fujian University of Technology. He obtained his master's degree in history from Fujian Normal University in 2014, and his research interests include the history of Chinese coastal areas and overseas Chinese communities.